An
Artist
in the
Garden

A Guide to Creative
and Natural Gardening

ENID MUNROE

Illustrations by the Author

Henry Holt and Company
New York

Henry Holt and Company, Inc.
Publishers since 1866
115 West 18th Street
New York, New York 10011

Henry Holt® is a registered trademark
of Henry Holt and Company, Inc.

Published in Canada by Fitzhenry & Whiteside Ltd.,
195 Allstate Parkway, Markham, Ontario L3R 4T8.

Library of Congress Cataloging-in-Publication Data
Munroe, Enid.
An artist in the garden : a guide to creative and natural
gardening / Enid Munroe. — 1st ed.
p. cm.
Includes index.
1. Landscape gardening. 2. Landscape gardening—New England. 3. Gardening.
4. Gardening—New England. 5. Native plant gardening—New England. I. Title.
SB473.M825 1994   93-30053
635.9—dc20   CIP
ISBN 0-8050-2718-1

Henry Holt books are available for special promotions and
premiums. For details contact: Director, Special Markets.

First Edition—1994

BOOK DESIGNED BY CLAIRE NAYLON VACCARO

Printed in the United States of America
All first editions are printed on acid-free paper. ∞

1 3 5 7 9 10 8 6 4 2

For Harry,
my co-gardener,
whose help and advice
made this book possible

Contents

Acknowledgments

I would like to thank the many people who in their different ways have inspired and helped me to write this book. My gratitude goes to Beth Crossman, my editor at Henry Holt, whose counsel is always stimulating, encouraging, and of many dimensions. And my appreciation to Caroline Press, my literary agent, who guides me with patience and dedication through the enigmatic ways of book publishing.

My thanks go to friends who have encouraged my passion for gardening with kind words and gifts of plants. (There are certain spaces in our gardens named for friends whose plants grow there.) I think of Alexandra Austin, Patricia Corbin, Joelyn Fiorato, Patty Gagarin, Renee Hack, Rose Hughes, Annie Miller, Butzi Moffitt, Sarah Seymour, Fred Specht, Cynthia Steinbreder, the late Mary Allis and Pat Daly, and many other gardeners—friends who may have wandered through here and left their impression.

I am also grateful to all those garden aficionados who have supported my spring gardening workshops. They confirmed the need for a book such as this and urged me to write it.

There are many professional friends, art dealers, writers, editors, and fellow artists who have changed the course of my life by opening doors that have led to new and exciting projects, exhibitions, and commissions. I am most grateful to Janet Ackerly, Susan Daniel, George Dean, Stevan Dohanos, Carlus Dyer, Rita Papazian, David Kidd, Donald Richie, Martha Scott, Betty Tyler, Carol Webb, and Charles Yeiser for their support and influence over the years.

To our four daughters—gardeners, writers, and artists themselves—Victoria, Antonia, Olivia, and Alexandra, my appreciation and esteem for following the manuscript through its various stages. They offered sensitive and knowledgeable observations on gardening, writing, and my pencil studies of our garden plants that illustrate this book.

I am particularly beholden to our oldest grandchildren, Thea and Julia, for showing their younger siblings and cousins how to step through our gardens gently. The sight and sounds of children playing among the flowers and stepping-stones is a just reward for cultivating gardens.

And to my husband and co-gardener, Harry, my depthless gratitude for all of his essential research, advice, and comfort over the last two years. As our gardens are a collaborative effort, so is this book. For both of us it provides one more dimension and reason for why we garden.

*I*n 1984, when my husband and I moved from a large old house to our nearby present, smaller, newer house, our plan was to simplify our lives: fewer possessions and less maintenance, indoors and out. We planned to enjoy the turn-the-key-and-walk-out-the-door lifestyle practiced by some of our more liberated friends. I have always been a painter, with an exhibition and teaching schedule that claimed first options on my time and energy, after my family. Still, I had usually found time to putter, making small herb and rock gardens and planting containers with the season's offerings. Because my husband's business kept us overseas for long periods of time, these little gardens always succumbed to neglect and had to be recreated when we came home again.

Our new house and surrounding acre or so of land, planted with vintage fifties shrubs, flowering trees, and groves of hemlock and pine, bespoke a thoughtless harmony and the benign neglect of previous owners. Ivy and pachysandra covered old flower beds, trees needed pruning and editing, and the lawn begged for attention. The look was natural and unassuming, assured low maintenance and few demands—just right for our carefree new way of life. Though I planned to make a small herb garden near the kitchen, plant some bulbs around the borders, and fill a few tubs with annuals, serious gardening was not on our agenda. The tree surgeon pulverized forty or so insignificant trees into wood chips, and the lawn physician began his ministrations. Spring advanced, coaxing the flowering trees into acceptable bloom and old clumps of daffodils and scillas to flower just one more time. I remember feeling rather complacent. Our spring cleanup chores were much easier here. I began working on my little kitchen herb garden, weeding out old ivy and myrtle and installing a lattice fence for morning glory and clematis to cover.

As we had planned, everything was relaxed and leisurely, with no sense of urgency. Gradually, however, several azaleas around the terrace of our glass-walled living room began to reveal their true colors, finally combining in a hideous tapestry of purples, magentas, and reds. Even by our rather easygoing standards, this scene was unacceptable. One morning, with no thought of the consequences, I gathered my spade, digging fork, and pruning saw. Within three days the offending azaleas and a few other shrubs of little merit were gone, and with 400 square feet of empty space to fill, I realized that I must perforce learn how to garden— seriously.

My first assignment was to plant this highly visible place before summer heat defeated me and the young plants. I plundered garden centers near and far, collecting herbs, annuals, and perennials to plant around the randomly placed slate stepping-stones laid by a previous owner. I accepted unwanted plants from the gardens of friends—no questions asked. I rescued plants that I found growing in the old compost piles and others that had naturalized along the stone walls bordering our property.

Within a few weeks a garden began to take shape, even to grow, and I realized how much I enjoyed being a gardener. I loved working in the sun or light rains in early mornings and twilight. I loved planting, transplanting, and rearranging my new plants. One of my first garden epiphanies (and gardeners have many) came while I was transplanting one wet and muddy morning. I realized that I had never played in mud before and that a childhood fancy was no longer forbidden.

I loved my frequent trips to the garden centers, deliberating and considering the merits or demerits of various plants. Watching my garden grow, working in it, thinking about it, had unexpectedly become a most delightful and agreeable pastime. I hung a BE BACK SOON sign on my studio door and turned my attentions to the neglected shade borders and old flower beds.

One plant led to another and one garden section to another, and before summer turned to autumn Harry and I ordered a toolshed to house the bags of fertilizer compounds, gardening tools, state-of-the-art gadgets, and all of the other paraphernalia that gardeners must have. Our children, never ones to be caught off balance, gave us a status-symbol garden bench and an English willow trug. And as for the turn-the-key-and-walk-out-the-door thing . . . well, that was unthinkable. Who could we possibly trust to take care of our gardens?

Within four years, we became the keepers of three herb gardens, several long shade and wildflower borders, and three mixed border gardens around the house. Our contract with these gardens implied a few hours a day of our attentions in exchange for good behavior and willing spirit— a reasonable quid pro quo.

I learned a lot from these early gardens and started to understand plants by handling them, planting, transplanting, and rearranging. I found gardening to be as intellectually and artistically interesting as any work in my painting studio. The problems and their solutions are similar: concept, space, color, texture, composition, and all of the infinite variations. And as with painting, gardening is experimental, each incident relative to the incidents around it. Nothing is finite. The course of a painting can change with a brush stroke, and a garden with the introduction of a new plant. There are triumphs and failures, constant reappraisals and editing. And while paintings don't grow or disappear in the night, gardening has a further dimension: the mysterious ways of nature.

However, during the summer of 1988, our gardens had more to teach, and I much more to learn from them. In spite of an unusually warm winter, our plants reemerged in the spring in good spirits. But as spring gave into summer near the end of May, gardeners were put on alert with warnings of the greenhouse effect and global warming. By July, my garden journal reminds me, we were sweltering in six weeks of temperatures in the nineties, rain forest humidity levels, and severe drought. Our many hours spent watering, staking, spraying, editing, and grooming did little to amend or even check the progressive horticultural chaos wrought by these stressful conditions.

In the beginning of August, unamused and discouraged, I posted the BE BACK SOON sign on a garden fence and retreated to my studio to finish a series of flower drawings. Nature could have its errant way; let the fittest survive—they were all on their own. While I missed working in the gardens, there was plenty of time to ponder what went wrong and what could be done about it. As gardens reveal their problems, they also suggest the ways to solve them. Our gardens suggested that we "simplify." The guidelines were practical and ecologically considerate. First, the "invaders," planted for instant gratification and requiring constant surveillance, had to go. Next, plants that need spraying to deter pests and diseases were no longer worthy of our garden space or our time. Temperamental annuals, the exotics from foreign climes—clearly not happy in our New England summers—would not be invited back again. As watering is ecologically unsound and time-consuming, thirsty plants, intolerant of dry spells, and plants with Mediterranean airs (some of my favorite herbs) would be dismissed or treated as annuals in containers.

Prolific self-sowers and stake-dependent plants and those with unattractive foliage and midsummer departure schedules were no longer welcome. And no more plants that bloom only half the time that their purveyors claim and then just stand there, not doing anything.

With September and cooler weather, our enthusiasm returned with a surge of confidence in our decision to simplify. Though it meant complete renovation, a sort of triage, we went back to our gardens and sorted out the wounded from the survivors of that infamous summer. During the fall and following spring we filled the gaps with divisions of the fittest and some of their cultivars. As the next summer came and went our gardens showed their approval of our decisions with flourishing, healthy, and self-sufficient plants.

This uncompromising upheaval proved to me that many of our disappointing plants were neither as hardy nor as self-reliant as their promoters in books and catalogues would have us believe. Garden centers sell plants grown in southern climates and different soil, and tested and raised in pampered greenhouses or controlled field conditions. They can wimp out in real gardens, and it's often not our fault if they don't make it.

I also realized that attempts to impose, or even think of imposing, those estate and show-garden horticultural scenarios and conceits described in five-pound garden books was unreasonable and silly. Color-coordinated drifts of flowers, long extended borders, and trellises covered with glorious tumbling roses, needing fastidious and environmentally unsound maintenance, depend on greenhouses to supply instant refill and crews of gardeners behind the scene to create the miracles. One garden book reviewer writes that "these coffee table wonders have done more harm to American gardens than any soil nematode or overdone dusting of an insecticide" (Keith Crotz, *American Horticulturalist,* August 1993). I was also beginning to tire of the relentless flow of English garden propaganda and question its relevance to North American gardens, considering the differences in soil, climate, tradition, and ambiance. I notice that more and more American gardeners and book reviewers are coming to the same conclusion: too much mystique from across the pond.

Most important, I realized that many of our survivors were indigenous to North America, native to our soil and climate, and therefore at home in a New England garden such as ours. I became aware of a regional style of gardening, spontaneous and natural, almost a seamless extension of our surrounding fields and woodlands where our North American plants (some of them, to be sure, colonial imports) have adapted and naturalized. During the summer of 1989, our gardens prospered and our custodial duties were once again gratifying, in accord with our original contract. Insistent visions of a new and highly visible ornamental grass garden near a grove of hemlocks became a reality. We enlarged one of the herb gardens, and we divided shade plants, which led to extended borders and new spaces along the back stone wall.

The following summer our gardens were invited to be on tour for a local benefit. We were proud of them on that beautiful September day. Their moment had come—each plant stood upright and confident, vying for attention and praise.

Several visitors suggested that I conduct a gardening workshop, using the gardens as outdoor classrooms and my studio for discussion. During the winter, working on the course for these classes, consulting garden books and other gardeners and redefining my own experiences, I realized that while something can be said for self-taught, trial-and-error gardening, there were also much needless frustration and discouragement.

Where was the book that addressed the suburban gardener like me with measured time and space but unmeasured enthusiasm for making and maintaining a practical and beautiful garden? The books I found were written by professionals for experienced gardeners, and assumed that funds, space, time, and labor were limitless. Suggestions and advice were often impractical, unrealistic, and overambitious. Where was a list of plants, horticulturally specific, for northeastern suburban gardens? Where was the book with simple one-two-three instructions for gardening techniques—no arcane advice or confusing diagrams or cute drawings? I remember desperately seeking advice and counsel in books and magazines, only to find purple prose horticultural evangelism, stupefying lists in botanical Latin, and promotions of maintenance techniques ill-suited to suburban gardeners with so many other commitments.

My gardening classes confirmed the notion that I was not alone in the suburban wilderness. And as one thing leads to another, my students and fellow gardeners suggested that I extend the class material into a guidebook for suburban gardeners. It would be simple, practical, and realistic, germane to our situation and ambitions. It should dissolve some of the mystique and eliminate some awe without creating more. Such was their advice.

People garden for many reasons and in many different ways. Some concentrate on propagating and growing their own plants. Others collect and specialize (roses, alpines, dahlias). And for others container or windowsill gardening can be their horticultural universe. There are many more reasons and ways, but for me it is the anticipation and expectation of an enduring performance by an agreeable selection of herbs, annuals, perennials, vines, shrubs, grasses, ground covers, wildflowers, and bulbs, composed in a natural but rational order.

I notice that gardeners speak in one voice from a collective experience. In France, recently, we came across a reconstruction, based on historical documents, of a Gallo-Roman herb garden. That gardener planted the same herbs that I do, around paths of stones, just as I do. Surely his expectations, anticipations, and observations, 1,800 years ago and a continent away, were like mine today. Whenever I make one of my breathless discoveries in the garden, I find eventually that it is in fact just ancient wisdom and folkloric truth, long observed by gardeners and recorded in gardening literature at one time or another. I like that: the link with the network of gardeners is reassuring and comforting. I am not alone. I like the collective voice that speaks of an obsessive and satisfying pursuit, as simple or complex as an individual wants to make it. Gardeners speak with good humor of the unpredictable and perverse ways of nature. They are concerned today more than ever for their own immediate environment, as well as for the global future and fate of the earth. They speak of the dimension of time, of the ephemeral and transient nature of things. They know that gardens are the passionate creation of individuals and have a life and spirit of their own. They speak of the numinous and transcendent quality of certain gardens.

Visits to some of the great gardens of the world have confirmed for me why gardening is considered one of the fine arts: the Zen gardens in Japan; the royal earthworks, parks, and preserves of eighteenth-century France; the Renaissance and Baroque gardens of the Tuscan villas; and the landscape parks in England. All are works of art, fine art. Then there are the great gardens open to the public such as Longwood in Pennsylvania, The New York Botanical Garden, and others in this country as well as Europe . . . inspiring and educational, with botanically esoteric collections as well as their native plants in regionally traditional gardens.

Every garden has something to teach, but the most inspirational gardens for me are those on a smaller scale and dimension, the personal, private gardens, the dedicated and obsessive pursuit of individuals.

I think of a friend's Long Island garden, an eccentric and inventive series of horticultural events, unexpected incidents, and amusing conclusions, staged over an acre or so. It speaks of a lifetime of fiddling and playing with plants and spaces to stretch the parameters of gardening and push aside conventional wisdom. I think of an island garden in Maine, where a friend has collected and assembled rare plants, alpines, and wildflowers that sprawl over several acres of woody and rocky hillside. I remember a verdant garden in France with beds of perennials and herbs wandering gracefully between strictly clipped box and yew hedges, punctuated with slender columnar conifers. An arch of clipped yew led beyond to flat wheat fields, ancient battlegrounds of Normandy. I think of a friend's container garden here in Connecticut, replanted and rearranged every summer with a marvelous exhibition of annuals.

These are just a few of the gardens that have been inspirational to me, for the personal vision and expression of their keepers: amateur gardeners who found their specialties and made their gardens through a nontraditional approach, without benefit of horticultural experts or landscape designers.

Our gardens are young, but in the late-summer evening when we watch datura blossoms unfold and fireflies and white flowers light up the darkness and the trees surrounding us become black against a luminous sky, it is a magical, miraculous place. It has a "numinous and transcendent" quality to us, which is all that matters.

I have spent two enjoyable years writing this book. Our gardens grow and expand and for all of their youth and inexperience continue to teach and inform my opinions, observations, and prejudices about plants and gardening. The buds, flowers, leaves, and seedpods of our plants posed for the pencil drawings between these pages.

Five years have passed since the rainless summer of 1988 devastated our first gardens. This summer of 1993, with only 60 percent of normal yearly rainfall and temperatures often sticking around 100 degrees, has been the stuff of a gardener's nightmare. But on this go-round we have seen our gardens not only survive but actually flourish. In keeping with my faith that our plants are indeed drought-proof and hardy, we withhold water except for new plants and container-grown plants. Sometimes when the temperature is overbearing and leaves crumple in the midday heat this policy seems cruel, but to shower precious water over all of the different gardens here defeats the purpose of ecologically sound, low-maintenance gardening, which is what these gardens and this book are all about.

After this summer I am more convinced than ever of the virtue and merit of native plants and making natural gardens. I hope to encourage others to enjoy this "obsessive and satisfying pursuit" and to assure them that gardening need not be complicated or occult. I urge and encourage gardeners to order their gardens to a personal vision and measure, in accord with their own ambitions and interests. And I ask where, other than in our gardens, can we gardeners feel such a sense of peace, accomplishment, wonder, and creativity?

Note on Plant Names

In this book Botanical Latin is the convention used for the naming of plants:

In the *plant lists*, plant names are shown as follows:

Genus (in italics)
Species (in italics)
x before the species name, if it is a known hybrid
Botanical variety (abbreviated var.), name (in italics)—where applicable
English cultivar, or variety, name (in single quotes)—where applicable
English common name—if in general use

Example:

Coreopsis verticillata 'Moonbeam'   Tickseed
  genus   species   cultivar   common name

In the *text*, a plant is referred to by its "conversational name," which is either its English common name (daffodil, monkshood, foxglove) or its Latin genus name used as the common name and therefore *not* printed in italics (clematis, hosta, astilbe). Only if a particular species is mentioned in the text is it given in italics (example: *Iris reticulata*). And English-language cultivars, where cited, are shown within single quotation marks.

Composing Gardens

Oriental poppy
and bud

A garden is an area where a series of related horticultural events are arranged—composed in a given space within certain boundaries. As with a painting, the composition and design are determined by the borders of the canvas, and all activity relates to and is defined by given border lines that inspire the scale and proportion of volumes, spaces, thrusts, and tensions within those limits. In art lingo this space is called the picture plane or picture format—the space on which an artist draws and paints ... activates with color, line, forms, surprise, and mystery. Gardeners compose on the picture format of their property with shrubs, trees, paths, fences, flower beds, grasses, ornaments, and buildings.

Gardeners and artists share the same concerns and problems of organizing space, which is clearly why gardening is recognized as one of the fine arts. Composing our gardens here, on our acre or so of land, is like working on a giant painting or installation. The old stone wall borders are the boundary lines—the edges of my outdoor format. Groves of pines and hemlock, the winding curves of the driveway, the flat brick terraces, and low walls create structure and lines along with the massive volume of the house. One form depends on and is defined by the others, and they are all interrelated. Colors, textures, lines, and shapes are as important to me out there as they are in a painting, and the old axiom that the whole is equal to the sum of its parts is never far from mind.

The straight borders, flat terrain, and square format of our property determine the location, shape, and nature of our gardens. Fortunately we have never had to undertake major earthworks as the overall composition, while conservative, is perfectly agreeable. Our job has been to remake some derelict gardens and create some new ones.

I think of each garden bed as one in a series of theme-related paintings. It must be harmonious and in accord with the entire property and its surrounding fields and woods. I would not, for instance, insert here, in New England, a garden of florid tropical annuals, a Japanese rock garden, or a dry California garden. I see funny gardens now and then, insinuated willy-nilly in any old place. Quite incompatible with their immediate environment, they are horticultural nonevents, dismally unattractive.

Good gardens are instantly recognizable. They make you feel happy . . . fortunate to be in them. A sense of mystery and surprise is pervasive. They have a quality of being right, a natural extension of their surroundings. In one of my favorite gardens nearby, a fine old nineteenth-century house faces a long and broad expanse of the greenest grass, bordered by mighty oaks, rhododendrons, and azaleas. Behind the house, a beautifully proportioned flagstone terrace, edged with a low stone wall, repeats the slow curve of a stand of hemlocks toward the rear of the property. Not a flower in sight—not even a black lead urn with the requisite red geraniums. This green, understated garden is one with its neighborhood and in complete harmony with the setting and mood of the old New England harbor village of Southport.

Before we begin a new garden here, we consider our available time and energy to keep it along with all of our other interests and commitments. While we do use a lawn and tree service, leaving our garden beds to mishap at the hands of strangers is unthinkable, and nothing is more depressing than a neglected or fitfully attended garden. Consistency of maintenance is vital, for without attention gardens quickly lose their texture and spirit. I estimate that our 400-square-foot herb garden consumes an average of two hours of my time every ten days or so. As gardens are a stage for dramatic biological and horticultural performances, some of that time is squandered watching, daydreaming, and thinking.

We try to keep gardening simple—it is more pleasurable that way. Right from the start we ducked onerous and complicated maintenance nonsense advanced in some of the gardening literature. The idea of digging up and spreading compost over the hundreds of square feet of garden beds was out of the question. And as for lifting and replanting spring bulbs after flowering and overplanting the area with annuals, wrapping shrubs in burlap for winter protection, serving our slug colonies saucers of beer to drown in, and braiding and knotting spent daffodil foliage, well . . .

Our gardening philosophy is one of low maintenance and no drudgy chores. Our plants have to be self-sufficient, self-supporting, and good-looking for most of the growing season. They are well fed, get lots of love and encouragement, but we simply don't pamper. Spraying is out of the question as I am not convinced of the efficacy of organic sprays nor confident about chemicals. Therefore some of our favorite plants that are uncomfortable in our northeastern microclimates don't grow here anymore: hollyhocks, delphiniums, lupines, and fancy roses. The result is that our gardens support a cast of disease-free, pest-free, self-reliant native plants with a few imports that have long since adapted to the North American soil and climate.

My co-gardener and I have over the years arrived at a comfortable distribution of labor for keeping our gardens through all four seasons. I love to weed and rid the place of invaders with malevolent ideas, while simultaneously inspecting the garden floor for other events, solicited or unsolicited. I love grooming, improving the look of things, removing deadheads and seedpods, withered leaves and overreaching stems, and curtailing plants that are exceeding my ambitions for them. I love making significant changes transplanting, rearranging, eliminating—searching for better solutions for certain spaces, usually wondering why it took so long to figure it out.

Harry cares for the Bonica shrub roses in a way that comes close to pampering; prunes and fertilizes the reachable ornamental trees and shrubs, spreads bags of mulches and bales of salt hay, plants hundreds of spring-blooming bulbs, and performs a variety of other imaginative and supportive chores in the gardens through the seasons in all weather, with the look of a man in deep meditation.

In locating a new garden, I usually make a rough scale drawing of the house and property, and with tracing paper I experiment with different shapes and locations. Sometimes the location is determined by the plants. Herbs need at least six hours of sun, and shade plants like a cool, filtered light. Many of our garden beds are logical and practical extensions of the house—outdoor rooms. In the summer with doors open the house and gardens seem nearly inseparable. Plants thrive in such high visibility.

From past errors of judgment, I know to avoid making gardens under trees, as falling leaves and blossoms mean a lot of extra maintenance, and overhead branches need a yearly pruning for more light, air, and rain. I know to avoid rocky, hardpan soil and wet areas with poor drainage.

Once having decided on the location, we visualize the shape and size of the bed by drawing outlines with a garden hose until something more or less in accord with our ambitions and concept takes shape. I have also learned empirically that there is only one thing about gardening that is absolutely nonnegotiable—a well-prepared garden bed. Once we have fixed the location and nature of a garden, we ensure its well-being by digging the existing soil to a depth of a foot or more and mixing in humus, sand, manure, and topsoil until all is soft and friable, with good drainage.

Thereafter should a plant malinger, I will know the fault lies not in the earth below.

The importance of preparing the bed cannot be overstressed. I have seen too many gardeners who have been discouraged, even defeated, by a garden of plants struggling to live in rocky, hard soil deprived of the kindness of humus, sand, and fertilizer. (See "On the Preparation of Fine Gardening Soil," pp. 43–50.) After the garden bed is prepared I usually think about it for a while, enjoying the same sort of artistic paralysis that besets me before starting a painting. Ideas come and go . . . there are infinite solutions. In the beginning I was disquieted by all the perennial border garden hype. The deification of drift planting in color-coordinated season-long blooms, as advised in so many garden books, seemed unrealistic and unobtainable for *me*, an average gardener without benefit of professional staff, a seventy-five-foot border (at least), and greenhouses providing instant and ready-made fill. Further, these books with long lists of plants in Latin, their pronounced English spin, glitzy photographs of old and established gardens in their peaking moments, and little charts with colored circles denoting plants—all were a bit off-putting.

Charting a garden on paper, preordaining and preplanning a garden and its living, growing, and changing plants, seems to me like trying to bag Tinkerbell. I compose gardens the way I compose a canvas, letting one plant or group of plants, their colors, textures, and shapes, suggest the adjacent passages with awareness and respect for the overall harmony of the garden bed.

In painting, one color passage suggests and defines the next and relates to the mood of the entire canvas. Choice of color is deeply subconscious and intuitive, often not a deliberate or calculated decision. Colors and their permutations are infinite. Is there really a right or wrong? We all choose the colors that appeal to us, and I am partial to pink, lavender, blue, salmon, orange, and yellow. If a combination seems discordant, I send one of the offenders packing or debloom it forthwith. I shun cool bluish reds in favor of hot reds, which I use as accent marks here and there.

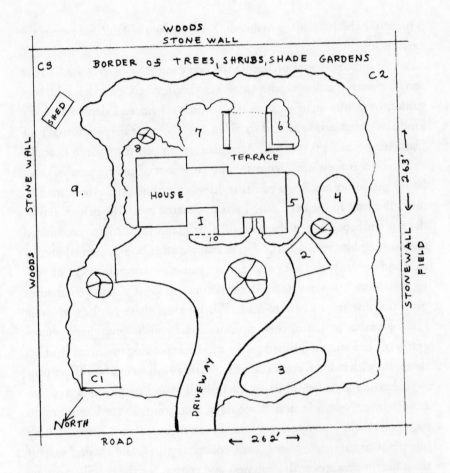

WOODS
STONE WALL

C3

BORDER OF TREES, SHRUBS, SHADE GARDENS

C2

SHED

8

7

6

TERRACE

9.

HOUSE

5

4

I

10

2

3

WOODS

STONE WALL

WOODS

STONE WALL

FIELD

← 263' →

C1

NORTH

ROAD

← 262' →

Garden Plan

1. Kitchen Herb Garden
2. Shade Garden
3. Oriental Grasses
4. Roses and Horticulture Anarchy
5. Mixed Border
6. Mixed Border
7. Back Herb Garden
8. Shade Border
9. Big Shade and Wildflower Garden
10. Shrubs, Shade Plants

C1, C2, C3   Compost

There are some color verities as applicable in gardening as they are in painting. Colors are defined by their ambient colors—no color exists in isolation. Red appears redder near its complement, green, than it does near a peaceful neutral such as gray. Complementary colors—those opposite each other on the color wheel—appear much more vibrant when they are close together. Neutral grays, whites, and blacks unify and fuse, keeping peace between all colors. Indeed, black is the great dynamic neutral—the synthesis of the three primary colors. Lucky is the gardener whose flower garden exploits rich black shade as background. At night when spotlights play over our gardens here and pierce the deep woods beyond, each flower assumes a jewellike quality against the darkness, the black of night.

For all of the to-do about color in gardens, many gardeners, including me, are more interested in foliage texture, color, and endurance than fragile and ephemeral blossoms.

Plants have basic shapes—round and bushy, prostrate and sprawling, spiky and arching, low and mounded, and with tall and short straight stems. I try to play these basic shapes with their various colors and textures against each other, by using subshrubs, small ornamental trees, conical evergreens, perennials and annuals, and low fountain grasses with their gracefully arching blades.

Through all of the gardens the silvery grays of artemisias and stachys along with the deep burgundy perilla, berberis, and heuchera, and the chartreuse privets, hostas, and spireas wander and unify. No one grows these plants for their exotic blooms, but rather to consolidate, to add dramatic color structure, and to create an aura of surprise—the unexpected.

I place stepping-stones and slates in some of our gardens for easy access and to avoid compacting the soil. Plants thrive, basking in reflected warmth, while their roots stay cool and protected. Stones are decorative and a few extra ones cover for spaces left by departed malcontents.

In composing a garden or sections of a garden, I often buy more plants than I will need and place them about in their containers until an arrangement seems particularly agreeable. Generally, tall plants take up the rear and the floppers sprawl along the border. As in organizing a canvas, I work from large to small, establishing the large forms and spaces before the smaller ones. Details and accent marks come last. In a well-prepared garden bed, most perennials growing in a congenial microclimate are programmed to live for at least a few years and usually much longer.

I make regular plant-collecting forays to local and regional nurseries during the growing season. They are wonderful research expeditions, and I depend on *Wyman's Garden Encyclopedia* for counsel. Wyman never spares the bad news that many garden writers, including the catalogue people, are likely to omit. Catalogue browsing is entertaining but sometimes reading all that plant evangelism bordering on science fiction is a bit tiresome. And I lack the patience to coax bare-root mail-order stock out of culture shock induced by suffocation in plastic and sawdust while being shipped. No, buying fully realized plants that one can inspect—see, feel, and smell—is preferable by far.

The purveyors of plants deserve a lot of credit for the gardening mania that has beset the nation in the last ten years, and for getting more savvy about regionally correct plants and offering new and unfamiliar plants bearing significant horticultural credentials. We are indebted to several growers near and far for their unusual plants, good advice, and inspirational show-gardens.

For all of our study, planning, and interventions, our gardens have the last word and let us know what to do next and when. In time, all gardens assume a unique spirit and texture; they are never static. Gardening and painting are similar preoccupations, and for me gardening is another art form to study and practice, as interesting and challenging as any work in my studio. It is different, too, in that I experiment alone in the studio, but in the garden nature is my mysterious and unpredictable collaborator. We work together on this joint project that will never be finished.

The Latin Thing

a rose is a rose
is a rosa

While Botanical Latin is the lingua franca of botanists and experienced gardeners who need a fine-tuned language to avoid misunderstanding, it is often intimidating and scary sounding to new gardeners. Long lists of plants in Latin are mind-numbing and exclusionary.

Mr. William Robinson (1838–1935), author of perhaps the most influential book on gardening ever printed, *The English Flower Garden* (1883), enjoyed a privileged position in horticultural and scientific circles of his time. He was a mentor and adviser to the world's most acclaimed gardener, Gertrude Jekyll, who joined him in founding the Arts and Crafts garden movement, advocating realistic and natural gardening. In one of his nineteen books, *The Virgin's Bower* (1912), Mr. Robinson, clearly a cranky old party, expresses misgivings about gardeners and their use and abuse of Botanical Latin. He has this to say: "In botany these technical terms may be essential, but gardening is quite a different affair, and for ages the effect of botanical classification on the garden has not been a happy one. Nor are they necessary; the names in our own tongue are as good as any and we are not prevented from adding the Latin name when necessary."

However, eventually we amateur gardeners come to terms with Botanical Latin in one way or another. I realize that with experience Latin does become more comfortable and sometimes even natural, and the gardening literature and lectures that I found relatively meaningless a few years ago are now much more comprehensible. If you grow a plant you learn its names—all of them. But I do think that botanical name-dropping among amateur gardeners sometimes sounds a little silly and even competitive and often is certainly not necessary.

So, in this book I list plants by their Latin names, followed by their common names widely used in this country. Usually in the general text I refer to plants by their "conversational names." To be sure, in many cases the botanical name is the conversational name, either in preference to a little-used common name such as Allegheny spurge (for *Pachysandra*) or because there is no common name. I have yet to meet a gardener or purveyor of plants who calls a marigold a *Tagetes*, a lily *Lilium* or a rose *Rosa*—not in ordinary everyday conversation, anyway.

Such are the inconsistencies in the world of horticulture. We gardeners take a giant step when we accept the fact that gardening is an empirical matter, relying on experience and observation, offering few certainties and plenty of ambivalence. Systematic and theoretical notions don't work here. One of the grandest dames of early twentieth century horticultural literature mixes botanical and common names in the same paragraph without apology. In a recent catalogue from one of the most prestigious plant emporiums in the country, the author, famous for his witty and elegant prose, switches back and forth quite freely between the botanical and common conversational names. What's a new gardener to think? Well, just be comforted by realizing that this wonderful enterprise, gardening, is not an exact science. In the next chapter I attempt to simplify the binomial system of plant taxonomy and make the Latin thing less esoteric for gardeners who are intimidated by the language bullies. I just wish that more garden writers addressing the average gardener would be a little kinder and include the common names along with the Latin ones.

The Kingdom Plantae

*A*mateur gardeners, unless they are pursuing a degree in one of the botanical sciences, need not be conversant with large-scale taxonomy—the scientific and orderly classification of plants according to their presumed natural relationships. Since I have over the years never really come to terms with plant taxonomy, I have enjoyed compiling the following evidence and trying to decode and simplify the genealogical credentials of the plants we cultivate in our gardens. I know a lot of gardeners who have created beautiful gardens and don't have a clue about the social background of the plants they cultivate, but I think understanding the taxonomic classification of our more popular, regional plants adds another dimension to the study and practice of gardening.

In the hierarchical scheme of taxonomy, the Latin Botanical genus name followed by one or more specifics is precision identification and distinguishes the plant from several hundred thousand other known plants in the kingdom.

Aristotle and his pupil Theophrastus developed botany as an intellectual science in the fourth century B.C., and worked out descriptions and principles of plant types and functions that were preserved by the great European monasteries through the Dark Ages. With the rebirth of learning and interest in the natural world in the fifteenth and sixteenth centuries, the studies of the Greeks formed the basis for reexamination and modification. In the eighteenth century, the Swedish botanist and taxonomist Carolus Linnaeus developed the binomial system of nomenclature and plant classification used today. He divided and subdivided the entire kingdom of plants into a multibranched "family tree" according to each plant's botanical characteristics.

My investigation into this taxonomy confirms that as classification descends pyramidally and the ranks swell to include tribes, genera, subgenera, subspecies, infraspecifics, variants, forms, hybrids, and cultivars, a noticeable ambiguity infiltrates the identification of plants, as botanists and taxonomists are given to reinterpreting and revising according to their individual observations or past precedence. For instance, in the latest edition of *Hortus Third*, Cornell University's 1,300-page compendium on matters horticultural, we are advised early on in the text that one botanist's subspecies is another's variant, all of which just shows that the natural world defies authority. And to quote the introduction to *Wyman's Gardening Encyclopedia*:

"Numerous attempts have been made to 'standardize' the common names of plants, but these names are the result of usage and many of the names now commonly used just do not conform to rigid rules."

In the search for order and control of the universe, botanists and taxonomists have divided and classified the plant kingdom into six subordinate hierarchical categories: division, class, order, family, genus, and species. Ranks are expanded by attaching the prefixes: sub-, super-, and infra-. Here goes.

Division

Division of a kingdom groups all classes of organisms that have a common ancestry and a related body plan. There are ten great divisions of the plant kingdom with four principal separations reflecting biological kinship among various algae, slime molds, fungi, moss, ferns, and the seed plants. Plants are ranked by the complexity of their vegetative and reproductive habits. We gardeners are concerned with the highest ranking and most botanically sophisticated divisions, the Polypodiophyta (ferns which reproduce by spore) and the Coniferophyta (conifers) and the Magnoliophyta, both of which reproduce by seed and provide most of our familiar cultivated plants. Within the divisions there are four main classes, more than eighty orders, and more than three hundred common families.

Class

Magnoliopsida (Dicots) and Liliopsida (Monocots), the two main classes in the Magnoliophyta, form a large and complex group of flowering plants belonging to various orders and families. Called angiosperms, these include those species that have flowers and seeds protected by fruit. Members of the Coniferophyta are gymnosperms, or naked-seed plants, which are the more primitive seed plants, reproducing by cones, with seeds unprotected by fruit.

Order

Classes and/or subclasses are divided into orders. The Dicots and Monocots produce most of our garden plants, trees, and shrubs. Dicots have netted veined leaves, woody stems, and flower parts generally in fours or fives. The seed contains a plant embryo with two seed leaves. Dicot orders include Geraniales (the geranium and other families) and Rosales (the rose and pea families, among others). Monocots have long tapering leaves, parallel veins, pithy stems, flower parts in threes or sixes, and embryo plants with only one leaf. Monocot orders include Liliales (lilies, iris) and Poales (grasses).

Family

The chemistry and the related structure of flowers, fruits, and other organs determines the family. Let's look at the aster family, of the Dicot subclass. Their flowers are crowded into clusters with individual small composite heads that lure pollinating creatures and ensure abandoned self-cloning. Daisies, dandelions, asters, tickseeds, dahlias, marigolds, sunflowers, and about 20,000 more species in over 950 genera of the Asteraceae, a family with global distribution, are all related by their flower structure, among other similarities. And the rose family embraces not only roses but cherries, strawberries, apples, and plums!

Good news! *The family is the highest unit in the taxonomic hierarchy that gardeners usually need to consider.*

The binomial (two-name) system was established by Linnaeus in 1753. It defines a plant using two names, a noun denoting the genus, followed by an adjective denoting the species.

Genus

A genus (plural *genera*) consists of one or more species. Large genera may be divided into subordinate subgenera. A family can have one genus or many, as does the Asteraceae. Genus names are italicized and capitalized but their English vernacular names are not. The genus *Rudbeckia* was named in honor of Olaf Rudbeck, a professor of botany who taught Linnaeus.

Species

Species is a major subdivision of a genus or subgenus, composed of related plants that can breed among themselves but usually not with species of other genera. A genus can contain one or more species that are variants. (Their names describe the variation in color, leaf, flower or fruit structure, or habitat.) There are about half a million known plant species, with thousands more being added each year. The species name is italicized but not capitalized, even if it denotes a place or commemorates people. Species names are usually adjectival and Latin or Latinate, giving a clue about the plant—color, size, shape, habit, and habitat. *Rudbeckia fulgida* is indeed shining and glistening. The species is the major reference point for the horticulturist and botanist, the working unit of the binomial system that identifies the plant as precisely as possible.

While the species is the lowest of the six major categories, the classification system does not end there. Cultivars (i.e., cultivated variety) are the selections from cultivation by botanists, gardeners, and other growers, who register them internationally under proper names, as trademarks are registered. These cultivar names follow the genus or species name in standard Roman type, but in single quotes. *Rudbeckia fulgida* 'Goldsturm' is a rudbeckia cultivar—one with slightly larger flowers.

A hybrid, the result of crossing two cultivars, species, or (rarely) genera to produce a new plant variety, is denoted by a multiplication sign (x) or, if they are a graft, a plus sign (+) before the name.

Though the common (English) names of plants are charming and folkloric, they are imprecise and unreliable, with many regional variations, and are not dependable in a serious plant search. Nevertheless, they

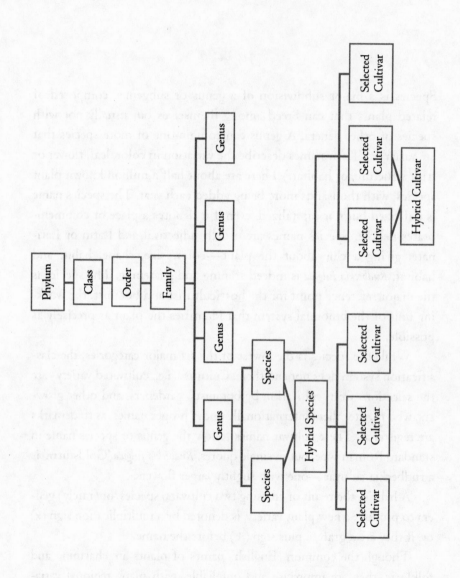

are widely used, as noted earlier, in conversation and commerce, including in this book.

On the facing page is a simplified plant schema diagramming a plant family and its progeny. It does not include all variations on a theme that has infinite variety. For those interested in more sophisticated research and study, there is no shortage of books on the related fields of biology: genetics, biochemistry, plant physiology, entomology, ecology, taxonomy, agriculture, agronomy, horticulture, forestry, and botany itself—the science of plants.

And now—to our gardens and the art and practice of gardening.

Tools and Other Paraphernalia

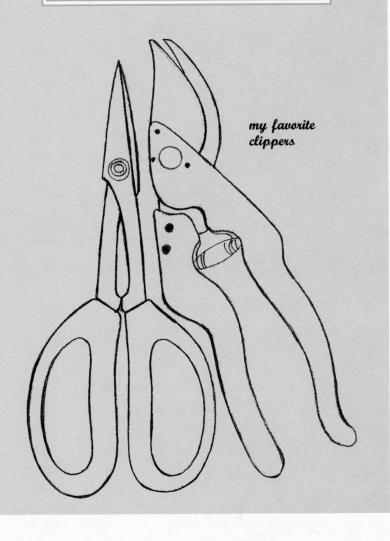

my favorite
clippers

G arden tools don't have to be hand-forged from a single piece of Sheffield steel and finished to perfection with hollow-ground blades bonded to aluminum alloy handles, sleeved with PVC with seam-welded pockets, curved for balance with cushioned handgrips, light and comfortable, never bending, splitting, or breaking, and furthermore, promising a lifetime of pleasure for generations to come.

No, they don't have to be, but why not? Craftsmen know the value of good tools, designed for specific jobs and fashioned of the best-quality materials, to make work easier. Often they really do last a lifetime. I had to break a few shovels, rakes, and clippers of less than superior quality before I realized, once more, that inexpensive tools won't do.

Unless one is working in small spaces, there are certain tools without which it is pointless to pursue the art and craft of gardening. I wish my co-gardener and I had started our gardens furnished with all of the following tools: border or digging forks and spades; an assortment of long- and short-handled pruners and weeding tools; a small folding branch saw; an assortment of metal and bamboo rakes; a long-handled edging knife; a small-bladed shovel or poacher's spade; some hand trowels and claws; and the finest clippers, known also as secateurs. (Most gardeners keep this singularly useful tool in a belt holster.)

Then there is the workhorse of the self-employed gardener—the two-wheeled garden cart for carrying, dumping, mixing, and carting. Children love to hitch rides in it. To be without this light, well-designed buggy is unimaginable. The old-fashioned one-wheeler is dangerously tippy, impractical for strenuous garden work.

There is one more thing—the handmade willow trug; a more sensible and well-balanced basket for lugging hand tools there is not. My trug goes where I go, carrying clippers, trowels, string, markers, tick spray, cordless phone, and lipstick. Because it is there, I actually put things back in it and don't have to crawl around in the bushes searching for mislaid gear.

Verily, gardeners do collect paraphernalia: tools, gadgets, pots, equipment, ornaments, books, and whatever else we can justify to advance our mastery of the practice of gardening. So be it.

We have any number of gadgets: five hose outlets and about a dozen various types of hand-held water sprayers, several long-handled water wands, and at least a half-dozen lawn sprinklers, too gimmicky to be friendly to the average householder. We fall back on the prehistoric doughnut-shape thing, which beats all of these newfangled hydrokinetic gizmos. We have this inventory plus several boxes of hose couplers, and around a mile or so of extra hoses coiled neatly near the woodpile in case we ever need them.

We depend on the catalogues for our top-of-the-line garden equipment. Most catalogues have 800 numbers and knowledgeable people on answering duty.

But there are certain items, such as latex, cotton-lined, thorn-resistant gloves (the only gardening gloves worth a hill of beans), that are hard to find even in the catalogues. We usually buy them, and my slip-on rubber shoes (with padded insteps for digging), in the garden department of the Paris department store Samaritaine, that old-fashioned, ten-story emporium hard by the Pont-Neuf. Its uniform department also stocks wonderful ankle-length rubber aprons. Not fussy, prissy little things these—they are designed to keep the clothes of winery workers dry and clean, and they do the same for gardeners.

Most catalogues are pushing their own line of clothes with an attitude—the used look. They are indeed authentically used looking—faded, torn, rumpled, and frayed—but still their designers don't understand what we gardeners really need, or take us or our intentions seriously. First of all, we don't need to buy pricey old shirts and pants when we can make our own from new shirts and pants. And no one—no one—can work in plastic clogs that drop off, get stuck in mud, or caught on branches. And who gardens in pigskin, goatskin, or cotton gloves? These ladylike things are the veriest stupidity: Water and mud render them completely useless. As for hats—they do get an A for women's hats, but my co-gardener finds his soft raffia hats only in the Florence street markets.

Catalogue clothing designers, whoever they are, could make our garden life even more pleasurable by recasting their notions of gardening togs and getting down to earth, with practical and realistic clothes to protect against sunburn, ticks, stinging insects, poisonous plants, thorns, brambles, heat, and water. First, they should knock off French work clothes, which have been around for centuries, and then they should (read "must") actually engage in real gardening with real plants, mud, and water. They should dig, haul, lift, saw, transplant, weed, and divide, and then we might be spared the ordeal of going to Paris to buy utilitarian garden clothes.

I have just one more suggestion for a well-rounded collection of gardening paraphernalia. I love to walk around in a light spring rain under my Japanese paper parasol, watching plants grow and listening to the sound of raindrops falling on oiled paper. When it is too wet to work, this is a wonderful way to be in the garden.

On the Preparation of Fine Garden Soil

a red zinnia

*T*he success or failure of a garden depends on the soil where the plants live and grow. Soil is the cardinal concern of every gardener—or should be—and is certainly the first thing most of us appraise in any garden.

There are roughly three kinds of soil covering the earth's crust: sandy, clayey, and loamy. Loam is a combination of clay and enough sand to offset the cohesive properties of the clay. It also contains considerable decomposed organic matter or humus, which provides fertility, moisture retention, and a hospitable environment for friendly bacteria and organisms.

With too much sand in the soil, water is neither retained nor absorbed. Bad. While a heavy clay formed by extremely fine and compacted soil particles is good for making pottery, it impedes drainage, becoming a hard, solid mass when dry and turning swampy when wet. Very bad. Summary: Clay soils do not hold much air and sandy soils hold too much air and not enough water.

Therefore we strive for a garden bed composed of a felicitous combination of sand, clay, and humus. Exemplary soil this, able to breathe, drain, and still retain enough moisture but without drowning the plant. Good soil holds the minerals and chemicals delivered by water, does not pack or clod when wet, and warms up in the spring. It consists of at least eighteen inches of friable, workable loam. The more humus, mulches, and compost are added over time, the softer and richer becomes the soil. Such is our goal for the garden beds.

Over the years, when we have enlarged and replanted some of the old beds we inherited here, we amend the soil at the same time without too much hullaballoo. However, making new gardens is another matter, and we don't even think of beginning a new garden without excavating and replenishing the soil. This laborious procedure is called "double digging." While those in training for hundred-mile triathlons might find this exercise agreeable, people like me who just lift one-pound weights several times a week at the local fitness center are simply not up to it, nor do we really want to be. My co-gardener and I double dug, enlarged, and replanted a twenty-foot border once, and never, ever again. Experience teaches. Now, when fantasies of a new garden become irrepressible, we call for our pal the rototiller man, his work squad and truck full of compounds: humus or compost, wet peat moss and/or a commercial planting mix, builder's sand, and the fertilizer of our choice. He will dig the new garden to a depth of eighteen inches, at least, blend the above ingredients with the excavated soil, fill in the excavation, and leave us with a beautifully raked new garden bed—all ready to plant.

Gardeners concoct their own soil recipes, and precision measuring is fruitless. The aim is to create a soft, friable, loamy, humusy, light, and lovely soil with good drainage. Gardening in good soil is an entirely different experience from gardening in rocky, hardpan, swampy, clayey, or sandy soil and hoping something will grow. In good soil, you know it will grow.

Guileless gardeners, such as I was not so long ago, sometimes feel pangs of delinquency by ignoring gardening book advice on soil testing. But as we are not commercial growers, I have never even considered assembling five to ten samples of soil from each of our garden beds, to a depth of six to eight inches wide and deep, putting the stuff in labeled, plastic bags, and mailing the lot to our Cooperative Extension Service (a service in every county funded by the U.S. Department of Agriculture). The revelations could tell more than I ever want to know about things out there.

I have also avoided testing for the pH factor, which indicates the degree of alkalinity or acidity in the soil. I don't want to know this, either. As most plants will grow, even thrive in soils with a fairly wide range of pH values, I feel this is one more bit of advice to ignore for the time being. As long as our plants appear healthy and happy, why troubleshoot or make extra work? I know that they live in the best soil we can make, and what more can we do? The best advice is to grow plants suited to your particular soil and region rather than amend the soil to appease inappropriate plants.

If a rototiller driver is not available to prepare a new garden, the following labor-intensive method will do the job. Take a digging fork, spade, and a big tarp with a wheelbarrow to the chosen site. Start at one end of the bed and remove the top twelve inches of soil from an area about two feet square, piling it on the tarp. In the wheelbarrow, prepare a mixture about half the size of the pile of excavated soil, composed of about one-half topsoil with one-half compost, humus, peat, or commercial planting mix and some coarse builders' sand to lighten the whole mixture and promote good drainage. Blend this mixture with the excavated soil on the tarp. Add the amount of fertilizer recommended on the package and then shovel this beautiful handmade new soil into the excavation, where it will be slightly mounded up because of what has been added. Then move right along to the next two-foot-square section. The finishing touch is a nice raking and a generous covering of mulch to prevent compaction and erosion from wind and rain.

The following buzz words are used by soil makers. Here I attempt to interpret them for other gardeners such as myself for whom geological mysteries below the surface of their gardens need not be solved just yet.

TOPSOIL   Crumbly upper layer of soil, darker than underlying layers because of its higher content of decayed vegetable and animal material (humus).

SUBSOIL   Reddish-colored, clayey layer below topsoil, usually sticky and compacted, which prevents roots from searching and interferes with drainage.

SAND   Soils with sand are coarse-textured and light and hold little water and few nutrients. Combined properly in soil mixtures, sand makes for a light and easy-to-work soil with good aeration and drainage.

CLAY   Hard to work or cultivate, impenetrable. In proper amounts clay is a conditioner, binding soil particles into granules that create good "tilth"—meaning a nice and crumbly texture, which is most desirable.

ORGANIC MATTER   The plant and animal debris that decomposes and becomes a hospitable breeding ground for zillions of small creatures, microscopic bacteria, fungus, algae, and actinomycetes—all mandatory for a healthy garden. Without these underground do-gooders, they say our planet Earth might still be just a rock-strewn place, spinning about in space and lacking its greatest life-giving resource—soil.

HUMUS   Bulky organic matter, such as leaves, hay, manure, and plant debris, which has partly decomposed and thus become nutritious to whatever soil it is added to.

COMPOST   The rich and black decomposition of organic matter (humus), and no gardener should even think of being without comforting piles of the stuff. See "Making and Mining Compost," pp. 51–55.

PEAT   Many soil recipes call for peat, which is mined in marshy, boggy regions and is composed of partially decayed organic matter. Used as a conditioner, peat keeps soil loose and improves drainage, aeration, and tilth. It must be presoaked before using and supplemented with fertilizer. Peat's days are numbered, however, as the environment's guardians warn us to quit plundering the peat bogs and disturbing delicate primordial ecology. Commercial substitutes, such as Pro-Mix®, are easier to handle, so peat deprivation is really not a serious blow to gardeners.

FERTILIZERS   A substance, organic or synthetic, used to make the soil fertile. See "Fertilizers," pp. 63–67.

LIME   Calcium carbonate is used to sweeten a sour soil—one that is too acid. Many plants are indifferent to its benefits, which garden pundits now think have been overrated. Further, lime encourages weeds and clover. Some plants, such as clematis and lavender, think they like lime but can be convinced to grow quite happily in neutral soils. Plants have to adapt to our soil here because I can't go around accommodating individual lime lovers with special doses of soil sweeteners.

We gardeners want our garden beds to have good depth, drainage, and friable texture, and to be dark and rich of color. Once established, soil only improves with time and yearly enrichments of compost, fertilizers, and mulches. Time and effort spent preparing good soil is never squandered, and the payback is renewed with interest every year. Just remember—soil makes or breaks a garden, and there are no substitutions or shortcuts.

On Making
and Mining
Compost

datura leaves

Gardeners compost for sundry reasons. Some say it is the lure and challenge of the methodology itself; others claim it is a mystical experience evoking resurrection. Well, whatever—most gardeners compost for the good of their gardens as well as their consciences. It is part of the covenant in gardening, and a practical way to get something very desirable for nothing.

Americans send 180 million tons of solid waste, every year, to landfills, and 20 percent of that is yard waste. More than 14,000 landfills have closed since 1978, and according to predictions in two decades there will be only 1,200 left. Enlightened communities and individuals are reprocessing, recycling, and composting. Noticeably fewer homeowners are lining the streets with black plastic bags full of leaves to go to the town dump.

One of the rewards of gardening is an increased awareness of the urgency of our environmental problems and the terrible consequences of irresponsible planet management. We who garden want to help however we can to forestall the global environmental disaster predicted in the next few decades because of the ozone hole, pollution, and ecological disruptions. Ergo, good gardeners compost and, in fact, can be a bit competitive about their product. Compost piles can be a sort of status symbol (some gardeners arrange them rather prominently in their flower gardens), but they do signal that responsible and knowledgeable gardening is being practiced on the premises. Composting is definitely "cool."

However, gardeners who regard composting as a sort of cottage industry have come close, along with the inventors and purveyors of composting gadgetry, to burying the subject in its own mystique. Let's dig it out from under the hype and nonsense.

For a while here, I thought the production of compost required high-tech, state-of-the-art composting bins, tumblers, and machines to chip, grind, and shred, along with thermometers, aerators, and other special tools. I thought one not only administered periodic transfusions of bloodmeal, lime, fertilizers, and water but also turned, layered, and sifted to hasten decomposition—a full-time work ethic preoccupation. Therefore, given our measured gardening hours and dread of anything make-work, we just dumped garden debris in several conveniently located places around our property and discovered, after several years, that our haphazard low-tech method produced our own private mines of rich, crumbly compost—ready to use.

Though estate and commercial gardening requires more organized and scientific composting techniques, we ordinary down-home gardeners can reap perfectly fine compost by piling our garden waste in any old convenient place, waiting a year or so, scraping off the top leaves, and digging it up for instant use.

Would that we had the time—nay, discipline—to lavish its goodness on all of our garden beds and lawns at least once a year, observing world class composting standards as devised by the truly zealous. But numbers daunt the faint of heart. The people who compute these things report that 1,000 pounds of compost is equivalent to one cubic yard. Suppose you wanted to spread an inch over an acre or so of lawn and gardens and let's assume the moisture content is around 40 percent. They say you would be dealing with around 65 tons of the stuff. Not a chance on this one acre. One just can't do everything. I feel provident knowing it's there enriching itself by the minute, the better to nourish new plants in our garden beds and containers.

For the benefit of my garden classes, we fashioned a shallow compost bin out of six-foot railroad ties—three six-foot square sections. Each square bin, one railroad tie deep, piled high with garden waste, produces a year's supply of compost for our pots and new planting holes. It takes about a year or so, with no aid from us, before the compost is brought by microbial action and aging to its best condition.

Gardeners with little available space for compost piles might consider filling thirty-two-gallon black plastic garbage bags with garden debris, a quart of water, and a handful of fertilizer. They should then tie and store the bags in a cellar, garage—anyplace. Cold weather slows composting action.

Truly maniacal composters can transform kitchen garbage into compost by investing in a kitchen worm bin and a few pounds of red wigglers. A designer-model bin goes for around fifty dollars, and fifteen dollars or so fetches a pound, or a thousand, red worms, and pays for shipping, too. If the instructions are carefully followed, kitchen garbage—banana peels, grapefruit rinds, and all—will be metamorphosed by the wigglers in the Worm-a-Way® bin into incredibly rich nutrients—compost— within a few months. This collaboration between householders and worms is clearly a sort of cult thing, with hot-line gurus assuring bin keepers with fruit fly problems that "this too shall pass." *Worms Eat My Garden*, a book by Mary Appelhoff, is cutting edge, and the magazine called *Garbage* is a no-nonsense digest of advice and information for avant garde waste managers.

Until things get worse, much worse, I shall continue to send kitchen waste to the town garbage dump. It is, after all, biodegradable, and my co-gardener does his bit by conserving our old coffee grounds for the acid lovers in our garden.

Planting, Transplanting, Dividing

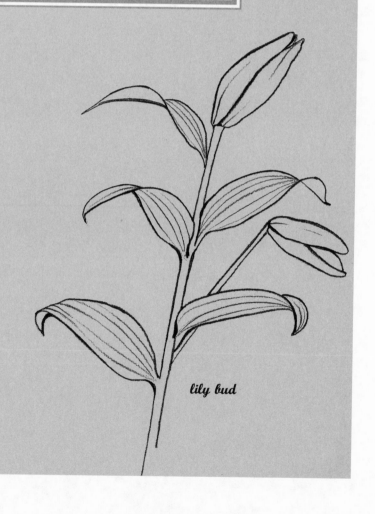

lily bud

Rearranging plants in our gardens is one of my favorite pastimes, as I am setting the stage for a new and different order of horticultural events to watch and study. I love to change things around—make space for newcomers, divide others that have exceeded my ambitions for them, and perhaps experiment with a super combination of plants that I admired, indeed envied, in another garden and can't stop thinking about. And changing things around is always fun, often leading to unexpected conclusions: new plants, maybe an extension or change in the shape of the garden bed. One thing leads to another and another.

Planting requires a certain amount of sensitivity and know-how, and is obviously the critical factor in determining the result—a successful garden or a horticultural misadventure.

If a garden bed has been well prepared, the following advice should help plants through the stress and trauma of being moved from one habitat to another. First of all, treat plants with respect and consideration to avoid needless shock. They prefer being moved in early spring, to benefit from obliging April rains. Late August is also propitious, with cooler weather and still time for the roots to establish themselves before the ground freezes.

While gardening reminds us to be kind and patient and to forsake plant surgery during a heat wave or drought, there are times when it is absolutely imperative to move things around or make room for a newcomer, at once. If I can't wait for a rainy day, I at least try to make my move at sundown. Most plants despise being uprooted, but can usually be induced to survive if well watered and sheltered from direct sun (covered by an old apple basket or garden chair for a few days).

These are my guidelines for planting or transplanting any plant, no matter the size, and they seem to be fairly foolproof.

1. I dig a hole, deeper and wider than the plant ball, and a lot wider if I am planting in virgin soil, under trees or around large shrubs. Plants need room to spread their roots and resent being squeezed into a hole of less than generous proportions.

2. If I am transplanting from one location to another and the roots are tightly bound and intact, I soak them in water, but if the transplant has loose earth around the roots, I get it into its new hole as quickly as possible. Then I fill the hole with soil mixture and water gently and slowly. The point is to let plants drink heavily to survive their transition trauma.

3. With a container-grown plant, I remove the plant from the container and soak the roots in a bucket of water until the bubbling stops. Then I cut, tear, or pull off roots that encircle the root ball. Plants that have grown up in containers are often suffocating and strangling in their own roots, deprived of air and moisture. If the root ball is compacted and hard, I loosen the soil with a knife or other sharp tool, which will encourage the roots to spread out into the surrounding earth, absorbing moisture and nutrients. Whenever plants falter, I often find that either the soil ball has become dense and compacted, or the roots for some odd reason were never sundered.

Next, I fill half of the hole with wet peat moss (it must be presoaked or it will stay dry forever), humus, or compost and/or a commercial planting compound such as Pro-Mix®. I blend this with some of the excavated soil and a handful of fertilizer, dehydrated cow manure, or Milorganite®. I set the plant in the hole, keeping the crown even with the surrounding earth, and fill in with the rest of the excavated soil, leaving a slight depression around the stem to hold water. Then I tamp the earth down firmly and water gently and slowly.

I keep transplants well watered for several weeks and carefully observe their dispositions for a while thereafter. Gardening is a matter of surveillance and observation. Is the plant happy in its microclimate and with its neighbors? Does it need more of this and less of that? Moreover, is it the right plant for the job considering texture, scale, and the colors of foliage and bloom?

Dividing Plants

Plants signal their need for division by outgrowing their assigned space and crowding their neighbors. Some plants, such as iris, are given to rotting and dying in the middle of their clumps and need division every several years. Another reason for dividing is good husbandry: to yield new plants for other garden spaces. Plants usually resent the intrusion and dislocation a lot. Having long since become accustomed to their situation, they give themselves over to my whims reluctantly. Unless I am in need of strenuous aerobic activity, I try to convince someone else to do this job. But when he is not around, I do it myself, equipped with a heavy-duty spade, digging fork, ax, saw, knife, and a crowbar for leverage.

After soaking the earth around the plant's circumference for about five minutes, I evaluate the situation, probing the soil for places of least resistance. Big plants, such as old clumps of grass and hostas unwilling to relinquish their hold in the ground, yield slowly to the digging, pulling, rocking, prying, cutting, and tearing. This job requires resolve, patience, and brute strength.

Once the plant surrenders, I separate the roots into divisions with one or all of the tools mentioned above. Sometimes the task calls for two people, each manning a digging fork, back to back. I think that with experience gardeners develop "good hands" and learn how to cut, hack, saw, pry, and coax a plant into sections (as brutal as it seems) as quickly and quietly as possible.

However, sometimes only a chainsaw can separate the concrete-hard roots of the big ornamental grasses or giant hostas. And yet for all of this hideously abusive treatment, we seldom lose a plant or a division. We replant with the same attention to details that we give new plants, and they recover from shock and insult and keep right on growing as if nothing had happened—so forgiving.

Fertilizers

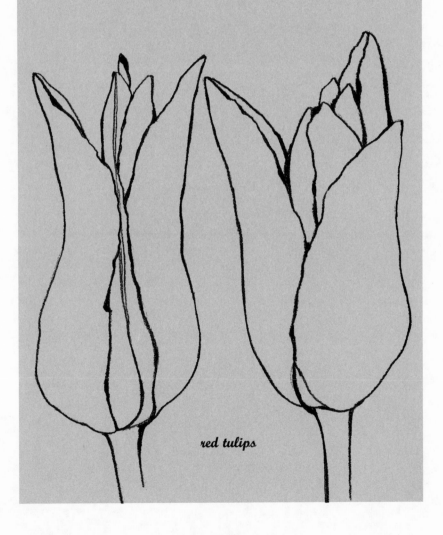

red tulips

*F*ertilizers supply the three essential nutrients to plants: nitrogen, phosphorus, and potassium. Synthetic commercial "non-protein" organic fertilizers derived from mineral deposits and "protein organics," derived from plant and animal sources, are available, with no scientific proof that one or the other produces superior results.

Commercial complete fertilizers come ready-mixed with explicit instructions that should be heeded; an overdose can cause burning, wilting, and even death to plants. The fertilizer people compound different ratios of nitrogen, phosphorus, and potassium for different geographical regions of the country. For our southern New England soil a ratio of 5 percent nitrogen (N), 10 percent phosphorus (P), and 5 percent potassium (K) is customary, and an early-spring and early-winter broadcasting seems to do the job. In some areas of the country with known soil deficiencies, extra numbers on the package denote the ratio of trace elements added to the formula. There are some twenty nutrients in a complete fertilizer, rather like all-purpose vitamin pills.

Briefly, nitrogen stimulates foliage formation and gives leaves their healthy green glow. With insufficient nitrogen, plants lose their vigor and the leaves turn pale. Phosphorus encourages strong roots and good flowering. A poor bloomer could be starved for phosphorus. Potassium fosters hardiness and disease resistance. Gardeners acquire a sixth sense about fertilizing, much the way parents do about nourishing their children: They need less of this and more of that.

The protein organic fertilizers are generally slower acting and longer lasting. Organic fertilizing is another subject that gardeners can turn into a career, formulating their own fertilizers from an assortment of compounds such as bone meal, cottonseed meal, dried blood, seaweed, fish meal, hoof and horn meal, tankage, fresh and dried farm manures, wood ash, and guano (the droppings and remains of bats, birds, seals, and turtles). There is also processed and heat-dried sewage sludge (Milorganite®), which we combine with compost in planting holes and containers. We also sprinkle handfuls around occasionally as we think the deer find the odor detestable. This summer they just stood around and watched us work but left the plants alone.

The true believer can call 1-800 I LUV DOO for trendy concoctions of high-quality waste packaged as ZOO DOO®—a blend of composted manures from pachyderms and other animals at the Memphis zoo. It is brewed in recycled cement mixers and packaged in stylish cloth bags—two pounds for around eight dollars. KRIKET KRAP® is another voguish sell. Its creators claim to have a customer list of 20,000 devoted souls, consuming four or five tons of the stuff every week. The brand name was only recently granted a listing in the Atlanta phone book. With such a devoted following, an 800 number can't be far behind.

Arguably, the fertilizer-with-the-most-cachet award goes to an outfit in Fayetteville, Arkansas, that mines and packages vintage bat guano from circa A.D. 1000. The guano miners feel they have gotten a raw deal in the marketplace as they can't compete with the big chemical companies that control the information reaching most consumers, partly by multimillion-dollar funding of agricultural schools. However, the guano miners think the tide is turning in their favor as more people realize the dangers of pollution by chemicals. Yet with 25 to 30 million acres of cultivated lawn in America, most of it chemical dependent, the turning tide may be almost imperceptible for some time.

If I ever have a cameo garden, I will treat it to the best bat guano money can buy.

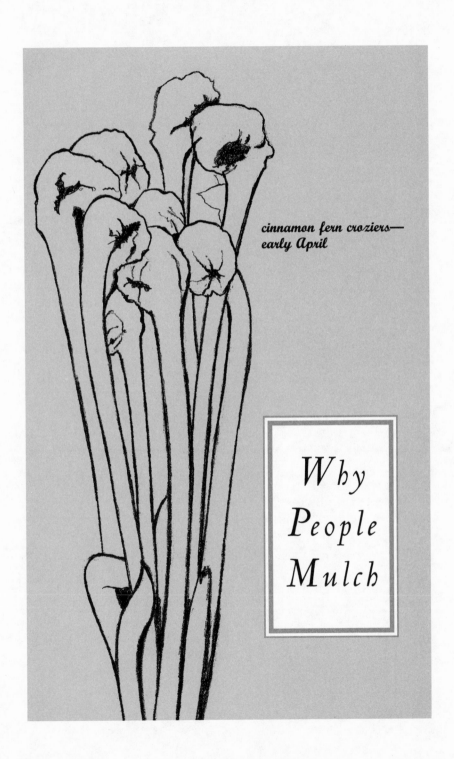

cinnamon fern croziers—
early April

Why People Mulch

Mulches conserve moisture and nutrients, reduce erosion, keep plants clean, discourage weeds, keep soil temperatures even, and their additional organic materials provide therapeutic benefits to the soil.

Some gardeners think mulches are too suburban and corporate looking (could it be the tasteless exhibition of plants that offends rather than the mulch?), but I think a distribution of handsome bark mulch gives a finished and unified look to garden beds. It is certainly more attractive than baked and parched earth.

For garden beds where we haven't cultivated a living mulch of ground covers to wander around under plants and shrubs, we lay down a three-inch layer of bark nuggets around the end of May when the volunteers (seedlings that have a will and purpose of their own) have signaled their ambitions for the season. Mulching before then could flatten their enthusiasm, and our gardens would be a lesser place without their vagarious ways. Our plants are fairly well established by then and require little watering during the summer months unless we enter a period of prolonged drought. Mulches help prevent the soil from heating up and drying out and keep plant roots cool. We use fir, pine, or redwood nuggets or chips. They are easy to buy and easy to apply. One manufacturer's chip is another's nugget, so inspection before buying is worthwhile.

We use small one-inch bark nuggets (chips) for the gardens immediately around the house and the coarser two-inch chips (nuggets) for the shade and wildflower gardens farther away.

Some mulch recommendations in gardening books are unconscionable. Grass clippings and peat moss, for instance, are difficult to apply and maintain, are ghastly looking, and are potentially dangerous for the soil itself. Cocoa and buckwheat hulls are ditsy little things commonly used in hybrid tea rose exhibitions. They molder, mildew, and scatter about in wind and rain and are absolutely not suitable for real gardens.

Shredded tree leaves make a fabulous-looking natural mulch, but their manufacture calls for a considerable expenditure of time running one more whining power machine to pollute the environment with noise and fumes.

We have several rather weedy and overgrown patches around the borders of our property that we have always slighted. They are shady, rock-strewn places where I don't especially like to work or care to spend money having professionals remedy the situation, only to leave us with a new maintenance problem. Planting out with a suitable ground cover and ignoring the places afterward is the most practical solution. With that end in view, we pulled all the weeds and mulched the places with several layers of newspapers and fall leaves, which seems to have halted incipient vegetation. We can now plant good old reliable pachysandra and be done with it. Our first attempt to suffocate unwanted vegetation with black plastic failed; it simply set up a greenhouse environment and a year later we were back to go.

Winter mulching is as important as summer mulching. It keeps soil temperatures from fluctuating wildly in early-spring thaws, reducing the possibility of new root growths being clobbered by a late freeze. It also prevents frost heaves and damage from the drying winds of spring.

After we have thoroughly cleaned the gardens of fall leaves and the ground has frozen and the garden creatures have made their winter quarters, we spread several inches of salt marsh hay and evergreen boughs from the Christmas tree. Salt hay is seed-free, provides insulation, and adds nourishment and tilth to the soil as it decomposes. Snow, of course, is the perfect mulch, but we can little depend on nature for a constant and adequate supply.

During the month of March, we remove the salt hay gently, ever so gently, so as not to break any tender, green stems underneath. Thanks to this protection the plants have been shielded and coddled, and the young shoots, liberated from their winter blanket and quickened by the spring sun and warm air, just start growing. Once more, down on our hands and knees, removing salt hay, we witness the miracle of renewal, one of the perks of spring gardening.

The Seed Factor

poppy seed pods
and bud

*S*haded from the summer sun under a soft Italian raffia hat, my co-gardener is in the "rose garden" tending his six-foot 'Bonica' shrubs and his fancy, relatively care-free David Austins. It is obvious from his painstaking and deliberate attention to detail how much he enjoys the assignment. He doesn't clip just any old place but studies the problem and makes diagonal cuts about a quarter of an inch above an outside-facing triple-leaf shoot (hoping for a new bloom to form this season). He removes diseased leaves and old blooms and squishes Japanese beetles besotted by the nectar of his roses. He stands waist deep in flowers. The hours pass. I think men garden with less urgency than women do.

Rose garden is a misnomer for this octagonal island garden floating on the lawn to the side of the house, for there are also large clumps of perennials: giant nepetas, white bleeding hearts, Siberian iris, lady's-mantle, tarragon, lamb's ears, meadow sage, the gray artemisia, Madonna lilies, and caryopteris. Moreover, I cast fertile seeds upon this stage to assort themselves indiscriminately around, under, and between the perennials. Forget-me-nots,

Johnny-jump-ups, columbines, feverfew, mulleins, foxgloves, poppies, love-in-a-mist, cleomes, and nicotianas appear by the beginning of May, and the garden floor becomes a higgledy-piggledy of seedlings jostling for position.

The Iceland, California, and blue-ruffled lettuce-leaf poppies covet the showiest places, forget-me-nots bloom in great mounds under the roses and between the lady's-mantles, and foxgloves send their stalks straight up from their compound nest of leaves. Love-in-a-mist reveals its delicate threadlike bracts, nicotianas gather in groups with columbines, and cleomes jockey into position for their summer takeover after others spend themselves. Little Johnny-jump-ups hide under the motherly blue blossoms of the giant nepetas and the yellow swags of lady's-mantle. Mulleins spread their huge furry leaves to reserve their air space in the back of the garden, and the roses droop with the weight of their blooms.

Horticultural anarchy? Indeed, but imposing control and order over such a spectacular congregation would be absurd. The purpose of this garden is to see what will happen next and with what imagination and ingenuity my cast seeds will sort themselves out. Yes, I know the undisciplined look is not for everyone and I admit there are moments when— oh well, never mind. But then I look at the crowds of poppies standing up in the sun—ethereal with their transparent scarlet or salmon-colored tissue-paper blooms and pale green, round seedpods straight up over ruffled blue leaves; to pluck out even one plant during this exuberant, unruly, and transitory flower show is unthinkable.

They all appear in May and most blossom in June, and when the blooms dwindle off I finally intervene with encouragement from my co-gardener, the rosarian, who has been waiting patiently to reach his roses without treading on my poppies. I clean up and groom, making spaces for the oncoming cleome and nicotiana seedlings by cutting back the spring-blooming foxgloves, columbines, forget-me-nots, and poppies. I leave some flowers to form seedpods, and in midsummer I cast those seeds for next year's show. Under natural conditions seeds fall from the parent plant to lie among fallen leaves and loose soil. They are naturally stratified or frozen over the winter, and germination starts with warm spring sun and rains.

I am more prudent about seed casting in our other gardens, and more disciplined about editing and thinning out. You have to impose order somewhere. I start nasturtium, morning glory, and sunflower seeds indoors in peat pots to set out when they are big enough to withstand the odd footfall. (Nasturtium seeds are hard and must be soaked in water overnight to help germination.) When the seedlings are about six inches high they are planted in containers or directly in the soil. Nasturtiums go in containers, the better to isolate the aphids they always attract; morning glories climb over clematis on a trellis; and we send the sunflowers to stand behind the big ornamental grasses in the grass garden.

Other than seed casting with or without discrimination, the other propagating methods I use sometimes are cuttings, division, and layering. Cuttings are easy with soft-stemmed plants such as geraniums and impatiens. I cut a stem off the mother plant, stick it in the ground, and water regularly until it starts to grow. Layering is a piece of cake. Pull a lower branch from a woody-stemmed perennial to the earth, nick it gently, cover the nicked part with soil, and hold it down with a forked branch for a month or so until roots develop. Eventually the baby plant can be cleaved from its parent. Dividing is the quickest and easiest way to get new plants. See "Planting, Transplanting, Dividing," pp. 57–62.

Some gardeners propagate under lights and controlled conditions indoors, which is economically practical for large-scale planting or for cultivating rare and unusual plants. This is another aspect of gardening, one that requires a commitment to the intensive care and nurturing of little plants with lots of patience and skill. Essential to the success of this enterprise is a knowledgeable and responsible plant nanny should one decide to run away from home for a while; otherwise the precious wee dicots could perish from neglect and abuse.

Buy seeds from reliable merchants. Mail-order houses allegedly have the freshest, rarest, and most newly improved stock. Besides, seed ordering mitigates midwinter gloom, that frigid time of semihibernation when snow still covers the garden beds.

Collecting and sowing seed from your garden plants is good husbandry. I dry seeds on newspapers in an airy room for about a week and store them in a film cartridge or other small container in the refrigerator.

Years ago a friend gave me a little vial of seeds with advice to throw them on the snow in March. I think of my friend often and fondly with a lot of admiration for giving our gardens my favorite flowers—the ephemeral, gossamer poppies. Now I give poppy seeds to admiring visitors—just one of the nice things about gardening, passing seed from friend to friend.

Bugs

lady bug, grazing

*I*n our beginning years here, I had recurring nightmares about the garden being wiped out by bugs—nameless, fierce, multiwinged, multilegged, flying, crawling, slithering, devouring bugs—or even more dreadful, by some sort of invisible airborne virus or underground fungus. My fears were compounded by garden literature (indeed, whole books devoted to bugs and plagues) advising me, the new gardener, to keep a watchful eye for early stages of infestation and infection—eeks! Well, it has never happened. Maybe a squadron or two of Japanese beetles or a colony of whiteflies invade once in a while, but that's about it—no big deal other than a few ravaged blossoms and droopy leaves.

Garden stores stock killer compounds by the shelfload should the plague ever come, but considering the lack of information about short- or long-term effects of chemicals on humans, animals, birds, insects, and the soil and atmosphere, counterattacking with sprays, powders, pellets, or solutions containing malathion, Diazinon®, Benlate®, acephate, captan, et al., is unthinkable.

Bees labor here from sunup to sundown and appear oblivious to my presence in the garden. Such honest, industrious, and determined creatures, bees, droning on while they work the garden over, and I am thankful that I am not allergic to their stings. However, I would not assume rights of dominion by attempting to stake the physostegia, say, nor would I groom the carpets of thyme or any other plant while they are nectar-plundering. With the patience and wisdom born of experience, I wait until sundown to do certain chores, after they all fly away home. Nor do I trifle with the wasp family. I think they are scary and they don't have a clue what they are going to do next. I give these erratic and unpredictable creatures their air space without argument.

Whiteflies are a nuisance outdoors as well as in a greenhouse. I make an exception here to my stand against chemicals by treating several of my prize-winning, classy, and expensive topiaries and standards to a dose of systemic Bonide® crystals every three months, which really does deter whiteflies on indoor plants. Outdoors, if the things begin to swarm, their breeding ground can be expunged by ruthless plant grooming and cutting back, to promote air circulation and alleviate dampness. Burn infested plant parts; never put diseased plant parts in compost. If any of my pampered indoor plants—ivy, rosemary, heliotrope, bay, and myrtle—attract mites, mealybugs, scale, aphids, or any other repulsive thing, I forfeit them. There are so many interesting plants to experiment with, why spend time coaxing lollygaggers?

My experience with folkloric recipes has been iffy at best: too fussy, slow acting, or ineffective. Infestations need repeated applications, and I just never really get rid of the problem; and using chemicals, other than systemic granules on container plants, is out of the question. Removing plant debris, dead leaves, spent blossoms, and sick plants helps to prevent invasions of diseases and pests: no place for the little blighters to hang out and reproduce themselves. And should a plant attract disease, virus, or bugs, I remove it, rather than hope it will get better; they seldom do.

One folkloric organic recipe that actually works almost instantly in the garden is to sprinkle cornmeal around a plant being savaged by cutworms; they gorge themselves and (so I am told) blow up. Also, the slimy, gooey slug changes direction rather than crawl over coarse sand and/or wood ashes, for most of the summer anyway. Anything is better than emptying saucers of beer filled with drowned slugs, that particularly distasteful recommendation from garden advisers who obviously don't attend to their own gardens.

There are lots of botanical and organic insecticides on the market, and gardeners find their way somehow through the glut of conflicting information and opinions. While I think most natural remedies are safe, I'm just not convinced they are effective, or that it is worth the effort in many cases. And that is the sum of my experience and attitude about bugs and diseases. I think the fear is worse than the actuality, and you can always send the odd bug-attracting host plant off to the garbage dump.

Think of all the good hardworking little earthworms, ladybugs, dragonflies, bees, birds, butterflies, and toads laboring to make your garden a better place and count your blessings.

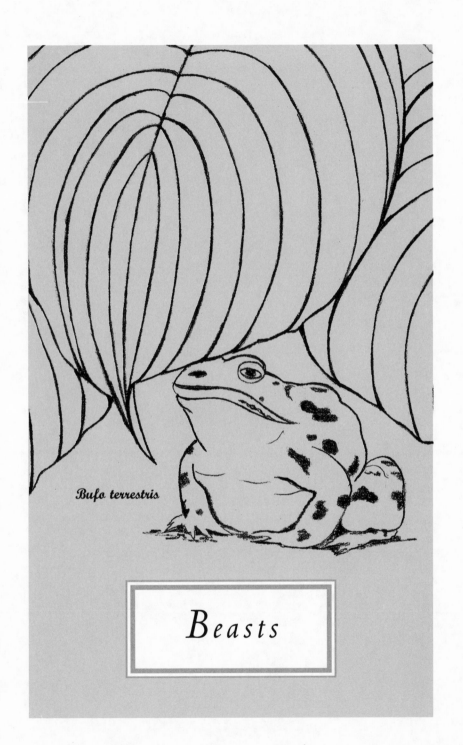

Bufo terrestris

Beasts

Our property, smack in middle suburbia, is a game preserve for small wild animals and an extended family of does and fawns. Their buck never appears, perhaps preferring grander, more bountiful grazing grounds than these. On the western border, the meadow beyond the stone wall (our borrowed landscape) is mined with underground tunnels and burrows of possums, woodchucks, skunks, moles, voles, rabbits, and who knows what all. The primeval forest to the rear of our property (more borrowed landscape) is a sort of high-wire playground for squirrels and chipmunks, our occasional bulb snatchers. All of them would love to have at our gardens and clearly just bide their time, skulking around out there, watching our every move.

One spring night we awoke with a start to crashing and banging in the attic—things being thrown around. A burglar? We were paralyzed, until we heard running feet and scratching. No burglar (phew!), just a damned raccoon again, possibly rabid, searching for a jolly nesting place above our very heads.

For a few weeks in April and May we load our humane Havahart® trap with bananas and lettuce to lure raccoons that would inhabit our attic, as well as possums and woodchucks that would level off our plants. Once they enter the steel precincts of the trap they are doomed to go for a little ride in the country, where they are ejected oh so far from home. Heartless? Not on your life—not at all, considering their temerity, chomping my precious plants to the ground in broad daylight even as we stand and watch.

So much for these four-footed beasties whose instincts and crafty ways pale before those of the bounding white-tailed deer. What gardener doesn't admire them for their graceful, arching leaps and noble posturing and loathe them for their voracious and destructive gluttony? And now, with the fear of ticks carrying Lyme disease, which deer host and spread, the creatures have become intolerable.

The problems of deer browse and its devastating horticultural damage are well documented. I have the utmost sympathy for gardeners who must fence their gardens with electric wires or, worse, abandon some or all of them rather than garden in a state of permanent vigilance and despair. In our neighborhood no one grows tulips anymore or yew or azaleas. What's the point, so quickly are they shredded? We would like to have a small vegetable garden, but gardening behind electric fortification seems to defeat its purpose and spirit.

Little will be done soon to resolve the deer population problem. It is political dynamite, with the animal rights people facing off against the agriculturalists. So we might as well learn to coexist with and outwit the beasts as best we can. First of all, we no longer plant their favorite food: yew, azalea, and tulips. We defend our remaining laurel, azalea, and rhododendrons by draping them with the nearly invisible black plastic netting and sprinkling Milorganite®, the processed sewage sludge (with a smell apparently repulsive to deer) on the garden beds. We also have many strong-smelling herbs in all the gardens, such as feverfew, artemisia, sage, catmint, and thyme, and possibly deer find these plants offensive to their sensibilities. They graze on fallen apples, and a few unprotected and unimportant plants around the peripheries, but so far they have yet to savage our flower gardens. For this we are grateful, as we face the future hoping that malodorous plants and other execrable smells will continue to offend these handsome hoodlums.

But there are three wee creatures living in our gardens who can do no wrong, and whose antics I depend on to make myself interesting and amusing to my children's children: Toad, Mole, and Rabbit, the endearing characters in our family's favorite children's books. The young love to hear that Toad scares me to pieces, jumping out from under plants when I least expect it, and that Rabbit eats my blue flowers and then watches me as I garden, or that Mole causes my best plants to sink into his tunnels and keel over backward. Perhaps my children's children, as we sit close together on a garden bench, are humoring me by asking "and then what happened, Mimi?" questions . . . but I think not.

Composing with Perennials

Olivia's iris

*P*erennials are plants with soft, fleshy stems that die back in winter. The roots and crown remain alive to send up new spring growth. Most perennials are programmed to live (well, for at least two years!). The good news is that some go on forever.

Most gardeners use perennials in mixed borders with a variety of other plants, small shrubs, dwarf flowering trees, vines, ground covers, herbs, and annuals.

The perennials for sun and shade in the following list have survived with distinction in our gardens over the years, tolerating New England's climate and acid soil, keeping up appearances with minimum maintenance through long droughts, heat waves, humid rain forest conditions, and warm winters. Further, they are mildew- and disease-resistant, noninvasive, and self-supporting. It is no surprise that most of our plants are native—indigenous to North America.

Many more plants have come and gone here. Some have disappeared mysteriously or fallen short of their hype in our gardens. Some were invasive, sulky, or badly mannered, flopping about or attracting bugs. Our plants are privileged—growing in well-prepared beds with friable soil and good drainage. We mulch with small pine bark chips at the end of May after the volunteers have appeared and with salt hay after the ground freezes in December. We divide perennials when they outgrow their allotted spaces or separate in the middle of the clump. We scatter 5-10-5 fertilizer in late fall and early spring. The sun-loving perennials and herb gardens face south and west and need at least six hours of daily sun, while the shade plants grow in filtered light in sheltered northern exposures. Our island gardens of ornamental grasses and the so-called rose garden stand before groves of dark conifers and thrive in the protected exposure and uninhibited flow of air and breezes.

My selections are based on our experience in our microclimates, but they should nevertheless be reliable and hardy plants for starting or improving most gardens. Many new gardeners think perennials bloom all summer and are disappointed when blooms dwindle off after three weeks or so. Thus, experienced gardeners rely on interesting foliage, different and varied shapes, and a complement of annuals and biennials for color in mixed border gardens.

Study the list and cross-reference with plants in your local garden centers. Don't expect instant perfection or be afraid to experiment. There are endless variables and infinite solutions. Gardeners and their gardens develop a personal and individual style and harmony that with experience and age change and evolve over the years.

Gardeners become compulsive plant collectors, and just as one plant leads to another, one garden leads to another. Getting to know new plants, welcoming back old favorites in early spring, planting, dividing, transplanting, composing, nurturing, and maintaining are, as every gardener knows, the pleasures of gardening.

Measurements refer to height. Where no common name is listed, (i.e., astilbe, iris), the genus name is used as the common name.

Some Hardy Disease-, Pest-, and Drought-Resistant Perennials for Sun and Shade

Anemone x *hybrida*   Japanese Anemone

3–6 feet, shade; pink and white flowers on tall, graceful stems in late summer. Good spreader—an elegant, willowy plant.

Aquilegia   Columbine

2–5 feet, sun/shade; many colors. Romantic wilding, reseeding everywhere. Cut back after blooming—foliage reappears fresh and young. Some are native but they all often naturalize.

Aruncus dioicus   Goatsbeard

A star performer at the back of a shade border, with white astilbe-like feathery blooms in early summer. Tall and self-supporting, an important, substantial plant.

Asclepias tuberosa   Butterfly Weed

Native, 2–3 feet, sun; soft orange-red clusters, midsummer. Late arrival in spring: Mark its spot. Beguiling plant with lots of presence, little ego.

Aster x *frikartii*   Frikart's Aster

2–4 feet, sun; profuse blooms of blue daisies all season if dead-headed. Pinch back in spring to encourage branching. This plant just likes to have fun all summer.

Astilbe x *arendsii*

1–4 feet, shade; pink, white, or red plumes high above fernlike foliage. Likes cool, moist, mulched soil.

A. *chinensis* 'Pumila'—a 12-inch-high dwarf—wonderful front of border plant and slowly spreading ground cover with mauve-pink flowers.

There are lots of interesting *Astilbe* cultivars to try.

Boltonia asteroides

Native, 4 feet, sun; profuse bloomer, small white or pink daisies on vertical stems. Big spreader; just pull up to control.

Brunnera macrophylla   Siberian Bugloss

1½ feet, sun/shade; blue forget-me-not-like flowers with coarse green leaves. Good along front of border.

Campanula lactiflora   Milky Bellflower

4 feet, sun/shade; blue, purple, white; many cultivars of various heights. Good plant to experiment with in various situations. Cut back in early June to control height and therefore avoid staking.

Chrysanthemum x *superbum* (*Leucanthemum* x *superbum*)   Shasta Daisy

Native, hardy 1–3 feet; classic, old-fashioned garden flowers for sun or shade. Shasta daisies are good reseeders and emerge in unexpected places, adding a sense of spontaneity to the general scene in early summer.

Cimicifuga racemosa   Snakeroot

Native, 6 feet, shade lover, fernlike leaves. Tall willowy wands support racemes of creamy white flowers. Dramatic, with long-lasting blooms.

Coreopsis verticillata 'Moonbeam'   Threadleaf Coreopsis

Native, 2 feet, sun/shade; masses of yellow daisylike flowers on airy mounds of delicate foliage. Deblooming encourages more blooms. Super texture and shape for center or front of garden.

Dicentra spectabilis   Bleeding Heart

3–5 feet tall with a wide wing-spread. Shade, some sun. Arching
stems support tiny heart-shaped flowers in pink or white. Clones
itself willingly. Be prepared to fill in the large spaces left by its
midsummer disappearing act. A wonderfully romantic, old-
fashioned plant and a natural companion for the perpendicular
foxglove.

D. eximia 'Alba'—Native, 1–2 feet, shade, dwarf, ever-blooming,
mounded delicate blue foliage. Exemplary behavior and attitude,
demanding little if any maintenance. The pink bloom, 'Luxuriant',
is less elegant than the white-flowered 'Alba'.

Helianthus x *multiflorus*   Sunflower

6 feet, sun, produces masses of yellow flowers all summer. Nice big
bushy plant.

Hemerocallis   Daylily

2–5 feet, sun/part shade. Fleshy-rooted medicinal herb, from the
Greek meaning "beautiful for a day." A fanatical band of daylily
hybridizers bring forth new cultivars every day by crossing one
hybrid with another. From the thousand or more registered each
year, there is something for every garden someplace. Plant in distant places, as blooms last one day and then just hang there. The
dwarf golden yellow 'Stella d'Oro' seems more compatible with
mixed border plants.

Heuchera sanguinea   Coralbells

Native, 2–3 feet, sun/shade; long slender wands of tiny pink flowers waving over low mounded foliage . . . charming!

Hosta   Plantain Lily

Shade or filtered sun. There are over 600 cultivars of this wonderful, versatile, dramatic backbone of the shade garden, ranging

from *H. venusta*, an 8-inch mini, to *H. sieboldiana* 'Elegans', whose giant blue-green puckered leaves can reach a 6-foot spread in one year. Warning: Hosta collecting is addictive! See "Hostas," p. 170.

Iris ensata (I. kaempferi)   Japanese Iris
I. sibirica   Siberian Iris

3 feet, sun or light shade, spring-blooming. Good clumpers, graceful and longer blooming than the disease-prone bearded iris. Divide when center section becomes unproductive.

Kirengeshomae palmata

3–4 feet, huge, elegant, shrublike plant with purple arching stems and pale yellow flowers. Likes cool, moist soil and is a perfect transition plant for the back of shade gardens along with cimicifuga and rodgersia.

Lilium   Lily

The great hybrids—Asiatic, aurelian, tiger, and Oriental: 4–6 feet or more, light shade or sun. Take your pick of the garden stars—early, middle, or late blooming, any old color, fragrant and romantic, what flowers are all about! As the plants need to replenish themselves after blooming, plant the bulbs around other plants that will cover the spent stems. Divide bulbs to propagate. See "Lilies," pp. 152–153.

Liriope muscari   Lilyturf

1–2 feet, shade or sun; blue, exuberant, low-growing grasslike leaves, pretty spiky blue flowers in midsummer. Good plant for texture and leaf color.

Oenothera tetragona   Evening Primrose

Native, 2 feet, sun/shade, happy yellow, long-blooming spring invader, easily curtailed.

Paeonia Peony

2–4 feet, sun. Hundreds of cultivars to investigate—pink, red, and white, single or double; ephemeral and top-heavy blooms. A few established heart-breaking peonies lend a certain cachet to gardens.

Phlox divaricata Blue Phlox

Native, 1 foot, shade, some sun. Slow-growing, white or blue, long-blooming spring woodland plant.

Phlox maculata

Native cultivar, 4 feet, sun or light shade with white blooms and relatively mildew-free. Deadhead for continuous blooms. Pinch back in June to promote bushier plants.

Physostegia virginiana Obedient Plant

Native, sun or some shade; white or pink blooms on 5–6 foot stems; interesting long-blooming plant that needs staking in clumps early on, because once the bees find the blooms, staking would be foolhardy.

Platycodon grandiflorus Balloon Flower

3 feet, sun, light shade; small blue or white flowers on tall stems. Cut back early in season to encourage branching and avoid staking. Late spring arrival.

Polemonium Jacob's Ladder

3 feet, good shade plant; airy and graceful blue blooms in April and June; tall or dwarf varieties. Cut blooms to encourage more.

Polygonatum odoratum var. *Thunbergii* Solomon's Seal

Graceful 2-foot single-stemmed plant blooming in May and June. White-edged leaves with dangling white flowers. Fabulous shade plant, growing into well-contained clumps; stunning with clumps of maidenhair ferns and well-defined, empty, beautifully mulched spaces around them, in a woodland setting.

Rodgersia

Another large plant for shade and moist soil, reaching 3–4 feet with beautiful foliage and long-stemmed, astilbe-like panicles. There are several garden-worthy cultivars with cream, pink, white, or yellowish flowers and bronze-tinged leaves.

Rudbeckia fulgida   Coneflower

Native, 2–3 feet, sun, gaudy but tolerable blooms when others fade in mid- or late summer.

Salvia x *superba*

A catchall classification that includes a number of wonderful cultivars. Woody plants, 1–3 feet tall with slender spikes of violet-purple flowers blooming in early summer. A superb plant. Keep trimmed to encourage repeat blooming.

Sedum spectabile
Sedum 'Autumn Joy'

2 feet, sun; great copper flower heads in fall. Dramatic, with blue-flowered companions such as hardy ageratum.

Composing with Herbs

purple cone flower and
monarch butterfly

*H*erbs, the garden stars, are defined as useful plants: edible, medicinal, culinary, or fragrant. Both of our herb gardens are planted around slates or irregular blue flagstones, and we also depend on herbs in our mixed border gardens. No one grows herbs for showy, season-long blooms, but rather for interesting textures, colors, and fragrance, and to attract bees and butterflies.

Herbs give formal or informal gardens certain old-world romantic charm. Traditional herb gardens, designed with low box hedges outlining geometric forms and intersected by brick or pebble paths, require a lot of maintenance. Raised beds around a terrace, container gardens, or even just a small plot of three or four square feet gives a great deal of pleasure and require little upkeep. One of my dream gardens is a checkerboard composition of two-foot squares of blue flagstones and low-growing herbs such as thyme, winter savory, teucrium, and marjoram. I would play all the blues, golds, grays, and greens off one another and the dull blue of the stones. With a little knowledge of herbs, gardeners quickly learn to exploit their fine textures, colors, and shapes and to use them confidently in mixed borders or in their own special spaces.

Herbs are trouble-free, willing performers all season long. Some herbs are shade lovers, but most prefer at least seven hours of sun daily, as well as good drainage and average soil mixed with small gravel. They prosper around paving stones or between bricks, which reflect heat and keep roots cool. Let them have their way, crawling, creeping, and spreading into clumps and mats. Put pebbles in their planting holes for drainage and root protection.

Use herbs in containers mixed with annuals. Every kitchen door needs big pots of basil and mint to touch or pick as you pass by.

Herbs such as lavender and rosemary usually need to be wintered over indoors. Basil is an annual, and in the Northeast, parsley is better treated as one.

Sprinkle the ground lightly with bone meal every spring and fall. Mulch with small pine bark chips when the earth has warmed at the end of May. Mulching keeps out weeds, keeps the plants from being splattered with mud, and prevents the soil from drying out.

Woody herbs such as the artemisias, sages, lavenders, and santolinas benefit from drastic early-spring pruning to about ten inches, to encourage strong new growth. At the same time smaller herbs such as teucrium, thyme, winter savory, and rue need a good clipping.

Herbs are meant to be harvested, so clipping and pruning all season long controls shape and promotes growth and branching. We do not want leggy or sprawly plants.

Herbs withstand and tolerate drought, and with the exception of sage and its strange wilt they are fairly disease free. Some are poisonous, such as foxglove, lily-of-the-valley, monkshood, and datura. Only under strict supervision should children be permitted to eat any plants.

Many gardeners harvest, freeze, and dry herbs and concoct exotic brews, jams, sweets, and potpourris. They also fashion herbal wreaths, scented candles, and dried topiaries. There is no dearth of advice and counsel on creative and profitable things to do with herbs. See "Suggested Reading" (pp. 249–253) for recommendations on helpful books.

A garden of herbs gives one the ultimate horticultural pleasures: low maintenance, utility, varied color and texture, fragrance, romance, and beauty. Herb collecting can become an obsession. I have tried many and lost a few—I suspect our soil is too acid or we did not provide the right microclimates. The following list includes the herbs that thrive in our slightly acid Connecticut soil, and I recommend them highly. I would feel deprived without their company in our gardens. They are winter hardy, except where noted.

Herbs

Achillea ptarmica 'The Pearl'
Babies'-breath substitute; 1½–2 feet, double-flowered white blossoms. Old-fashioned garden plant, forming sturdy maintenance-free clumps. Cut back a little after blooming to get more blooms until frost.

Aconitum carmichaelii   Monkshood
4–6 feet, fall-blooming hooded blue flowers on long stalks with glossy delphinium-like leaves. Plant in clumps for easy staking in rich soil, shady places. Poisonous but most desirable.

Ajuga pyramidalis   Bugle Weed
Intelligent 10-inch clumper, spreading just where it should with glossy bronzed leaves and foot-high spires of deep blue flowers in May and June. Cut back after flowering. The lawn invader, *A. reptans*, is nice, too, but needs supervision.

Alchemilla mollis   Lady's-Mantle
1–2 feet, low-growing, exquisite foliage plant with sprays of fluffy yellow flowers. A garden star in England's kinder climate, but gets along here if due attention is paid to details, such as mulching over

crown, cutting back of flowers after blooming, and annual dividing in the fall. (It resents spring upheaval.) Needs plenty of sun.

Allium   Onion, Chive

2½–5 feet, from bulbs. Many varieties of allium: short and curly mat-forming chives, medium and tall garlic and onion plants, all with satisfying flowers that appear in round clusters, in various colors at the end of the flower stalk. Alliums deter insects and pests, besides being good-looking and well-behaved garden plants.

Artemisia abrotanum   Southernwood

3–5 feet, woody stemmed, soft, green, and feathery. Cut way back in spring to encourage sturdy growth and controlled shape.

A. absinthium Wormwood—3–5 feet, good gray filler for taller neighbors to lean on; needs occasional cutting to keep shape.

A. 'Powis Castle'—1–2 feet. Perfect low gray bushy filler. Forget *A. stellerana*, 'Dusty Miller', its shabby annual cousin. 'Powis Castle' is the grayest, bushiest plant around, lasting long after first frosts. Cut back hard in spring. Fabulous plant, asking only to be admired.

Artemisia dracunculus   French Tarragon

Gourmet's delight, this tasty aromatic plant grows happily to 2 feet in well-drained, rich, sandy soil, in full sun. Untangle roots every third year and make new plants in early spring, as tarragon roots can choke the plant. Russian tarragon is unacceptable; make sure you buy French.

Asarum europaeum   European Wild Ginger

Shade-loving, low (only 5 inches tall), and elegant with shiny green round leaves, spreading in well-formed clumps. Elegant, maintenance-free ground cover.

Baptisia australis   Wild Indigo

Native, 4-foot sun lover, with racemes of blue flowers on arching stems. Handsome, interesting plant for back of border demanding no special favors. Tolerates partial shade.

Chrysanthemum parthenium (*Tanacetum parthenium*)   Feverfew

Cooperative volunteer, 1–3 feet, appearing where and when you need it, in sun or shade. Well-groomed, bushy plant with tiny daisylike flowers, blooming all summer. Shapes up when pinched back. Let this plant have its own spontaneous way. Some gardeners think its pungent odor repels deer, and I am inclined to agree.

Convallaria majalis   Lily of the Valley

Romantic, charming ground cover (8 inches) with heartbreaking tiny white bells on thin stems shielded by elliptical leaves, all of which get tired by early summer. Let this one roam around under shrubs rather than letting it form a tangled mass of cast-iron roots in a proper garden bed.

Digitalis purpurea or *D. p. 'Alba'*   Foxglove

Long-lasting bell-shaped flowers clustered on 6-foot vertical stems. Essential for all gardens. Sun or shade. Let seeds dry on stems, strip and broadcast where you will. Next year's plants form in about 3 weeks. They emerge in spring from desiccated foliage and too often end up in the compost pile. Poisonous? Yes!

Echinacea purpurea   Purple Coneflower

Native, 4–5 feet, pink- or white-petaled blossoms around cone-shaped seed pods. Inelegant but useful for distant color and drama. Monarch butterflies pose on the pretty seed pods.

Eupatorium coelestinum   Hardy Ageratum

Native, 2–3 feet, sun or light shade; invasive plant, best left in isolated quarters or in pots in or above ground. Fabulous blue blooms in September; well-groomed plant.

Galium odoratum (Asperula oderata)   Sweet Woodruff

Ground-hugging (6 inches tall), pretty little spreader with tiny white spring blossoms, enchanting with forget-me-nots in shady places. It likes to wander, but its travels are easy enough to control.

Lamium maculatum 'White Nancy' or 'Beacon Silver'   Spotted Nettle

12–18 inches, filtered sun or shade. Variegated green and white leaves on spreading stems that reach around under more important neighbors, pink or white flowers.

Lavandula   Lavender

2–3 feet. All lavenders are romantic, fragrant, and grayish plants with southern European airs, often disdaining the acid soil and frigid climate of the Northeast. Put them in pots, winter indoors, or treat as annuals if you don't have a well-protected microclimate—facing south—to keep them as permanent residents. Experimenting is the only way here.

Mentha   Mint

So many types to try, in various sizes up to 30 inches, and another good choice for pots near the kitchen door. For gardens, invasive roots can be curtailed in bottomless plastic containers sunk in the ground.

Monarda   Bee Balm

Native herb, tall-stemmed (4–6 feet), pink, red, purple, or white blossoms in early summer. Good for back of garden with lower-growing plants to hide its mildew-prone foliage.

Myosotis scorpioides   Forget-me-not

Sun and shade volunteers with dear little blue flowers, 12–20 inches, in May and June. Enchanting with sweet woodruff and lamium. Let seeds dry on stalks, broadcast, and be careful about weeding out the new young plants that appear throughout the summer. Another one to remember in spring cleanup, as plants look desiccated.

Myrrhis odorata   Sweet Cicely

2 feet, sun or shade filler. Lacy green, fragrant foliage with flat clusters of white flowers in midspring; cut back in midsummer for fresh new growth.

Nepeta   Catmint

1–3 feet, bushy, fragrant, successively blooming plants with lovely blue blossoms. Several types to experiment with, all of them sensational and carefree, needing only to be cut back now and then to keep the show going.

Ocimum basilicum   Basil

Beautiful, decorative, and edible annual, 12–18 inches. Plant in containers near kitchen door to keep it clean and protected. What is summer without fresh basil for breakfast, lunch, and dinner?

Origanum vulgare   Marjoram

Sun. Perennial low-growing herbs, forming large clumps up to 30 inches high. Golden Marjoram is a nonflowering winner for ground cover around stepping-stones.

Pelargonium   Scented Geranium

This genus of the large geranium family (Geraniaceae) includes geraniums of many kinds, but the herbs I recommend are the scented ones. Sun-loving, exotically scented plants, 12–18 inches, many types to choose from; tender and perfect for containers. Can be wintered over indoors.

Perilla frutescens

Sun or shade. Much admired yet little used. Let loose this 2–3-foot fertile but easily controlled volunteer to roam in your garden and ignite vacated spaces with its iridescent purple and green leaves.

Perovskia atriplicifolia   Russian Sage

A beautiful subshrub, 3–5 feet with gray-silver foliage and panicles of lavender blue flowers blooming in late summer. Absolutely fabulous once it gets established in well-drained soil with lots of sun. Cut way back in early spring.

Pulmonaria officinalis   Common Lungwort

Superb ground cover. Silver-spotted foliage with blue flowers to lighten up shady spaces.

Rosmarinus officinalis   Rosemary

Half-hardy, evergreen sun lover. Winter over indoors if you cannot provide a sheltered microclimate outdoors. Given to sudden, exasperating demise, but easily replaced with new stock and optimism.

Ruta graveolens   Rue

2-foot bushy interesting plant with little blue leaves and complex yellow blossoms—a perfect foil for blue-blossomed curly chives. Sun loving. May cause irritation to skin.

Salvia officinalis   Sage

2–4 feet. Another beautiful Mediterranean requiring well-drained, sunny locations. Many to choose from, good container plant, and irresistible even though given to mysterious wilt and sudden demise.

Santolina chamaecyparissus   Lavender Cotton

18–24 inches. More desirable gray foliage from southern Europe. Needs a lot of clipping and trimming to avoid midsummer sulks.

Satureja montana   Winter Savory

15 inches. Colonial import from England likes it here and produces carefree, verdant low mounds with tiny white blossoms. Good edger; also does well around warm paving stones.

Stachys byzantina   Lamb's Ears

Lovely furry edge of border, mat-forming plant with amusing
silver-gray leaves and long silly stalks up to 3 feet bearing non-
descript pink blossoms. Well worth the constant grooming it
demands. Requires excellent drainage for good performance.

Tanacetum vulgare   Tansy

4-foot, sun or light shade foliage plant with interesting fernlike
leaves. Useful filler, fragrant, with tiny yellow blossoms similar to
yarrow. Worth the extra attention of staking and cutting back.

Teucrium chamaedrys   Germander

Small (up to 10 inches), woody-stemmed, glossy-leaved, well-
behaved little edging plant; happy in full sun and well protected by
winter mulch.

Thymus   Thyme

Any of these low, perfumed, fast-spreading herbs with pretty blossoms will do. Expanding mats cover hot stones, bricks, concrete,
and earth. Experiment with different types. Clip back hard in
spring.

Viola tricolor   Johnny-jump-up

Sun, shade, in any old place. These cute little guys no more than a
foot tall jump around, self-sowing, climbing up into taller plants,
or establishing their own spaces to show their wee pansylike faces.
Let them in to your garden to perpetuate themselves wherever and
whenever they like.

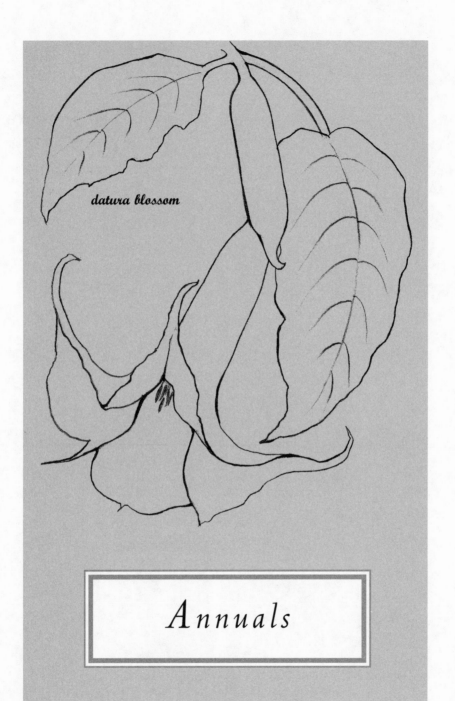

datura blossom

Annuals

*A*nnuals complete their life cycle within one growing season. They grow to maturity, flower, spend themselves forming seed to ensure their progeny, and die. Biennials normally take two growing seasons to produce flowers.

It is the annuals that incite plant snobbery, a posture most likely to infect gardeners who have developed a comfortable relationship with botanical Latin—a natural consequence of experience and confidence. Fair enough.

The exotic aliens from faraway places—South Africa, India, South America, Morocco, Indonesia, South Asia, and the American Southwest—with their tropical temperaments and splashy colors, horticulturally out of sync with our more subtle native plants and northern climate, tend to be an irresistible target for the scorn of plant snobs. I include myself in this churlish coterie, whose collective bias is perpetuated by those hideous gardens in public and industrial or commercial parks: geometric beds of marigolds, begonias, impatiens, petunias, and other annuals embroidered together with defiant disregard for any color niceties. In spite of the twentieth-century gardening aesthetic to stomp out bedding gardens, there must be a school someplace that is dedicated to prolonging this Victorian gardening conceit because it just won't go away.

Further bias comes from field trials here, when our gardens were young and inexperienced, which demonstrated that many annuals cannot take the heat or drought conditions of our unpredictable summers, turning shabby and sulky about flowering. And why should they not, separated from their native soil, weather, and tropical companions in foreign climes?

However, plenty of horticulturally significant, summer-hardy annuals perform beautifully in our humid, hot weather and enlighten our garden spaces, containers, and hanging baskets.

As I never cut our garden flowers except to pose them for a drawing, we have recently established a cutting garden in an out-of-the-way place, as maintenance will be minimal. We shall broadcast seeds and let them work it out unaided except for a soaker hose, a thin layer of salt hay in winter, and a scattering of dried blood to ward off predators.

Indoor seed propagation of annuals is feasible with unlimited time, patience, and space—none of which I have. We cast nicotiana, forget-me-nots, poppies, love-in-a-mist, and foxglove seeds directly in the garden and hope to avoid lethal damage from clumsy feet, forgetful digging, or birds and other wildlife. We do start nasturtium, morning glory, and moon flower seeds in peat pots indoors as they resent being transplanted. See "The Seed Factor," pp. 75–80, for further counsel.

I prefer buying instant gratification in fully formed plants from garden centers, which purvey new and seasonally appropriate selections through the growing season. Weekly plant-collecting expeditions pay off in the discovery of new introductions and an expansion of knowledge and familiarity with plants. Seduction once again by a pretty basket of petunias that I know perfectly well, from past experience, will have a silly tantrum and self-destruct is just part of gardening.

Most annuals like sunny places. The shade plants that do well in our garden are the reliables: alyssum, forget-me-nots, foxgloves, impatiens, Johnny-jump-ups, nicotiana, and pansies.

As annuals don't live long enough to spread their roots, they will withstand soil that is less than perfect, but good drainage is imperative. Deadheading makes the entire garden look better and keeps plants flowering instead of going to seed.

We avoid tall annuals that need staking except for the hollow-stemmed twelve-foot cosmos that no garden should be without, ever. We also avoid ageratum, delphiniums, dusty miller, hollyhocks, lobelia, petunias, snapdragons, zinnias, and certain asters and geraniums, all of which in our gardens have succumbed to whiteflies, fungus, rust, and/or mildew. I see no point in nursing unhappy plants that would rather not be here.

The following list includes our favorites—the climbers, crawlers, tumblers, and perpendiculars—all well-groomed, drought tolerant, disease and insect resistant, amusing, and content in our northeastern environment. What more can we ask of plants programmed to complete their life span in one short growing season?

Some Congenial Annuals

Chrysanthemum frutescens (*Agranthemum frutescens*)   Marguerite
   Woody branched, lacy foliage with daisy blooms in white, pink, or yellow. 3 feet. Sun. Dozens of cultivars—excellent in garden beds or containers.

Chrysanthemum x *morifolium*   Florist Mum
   2–5 feet, sun. This trustworthy standby, extender of the garden season with all of its tawny russet and golden fall colors, was just renamed. The new name is *Dendranthema* x *grandiflorum.* Imagine old garden mums getting such a swell name!

Cleome hasslerana   Spider Flower
   Eccentric-looking plant with multibranched stalks 5–6 feet tall bearing numerous pink, white, or purple flower heads; ever-

blooming and self-cloning. Don't stake, just help it back up from time to time or let it list.

Coreopsis tinctoria   Calliopsis

North American native up to 3 feet, full sun; red, yellow, or orange blooms on a bushy airy plant that needs to be sheared occasionally to encourage perpetual blooming.

Cosmos bipinnatus

Red, pink, white, and bicolored blooms floating around on willowy branches and stalks, which can grow to 15 feet—a sensational summer spectacle. This one must be staked or summer winds and rains will bend and break its brittle hollow branches.

Datura metel   Horn of Plenty

Tender exotic can be coaxed to perform and even reseed itself in protected microclimates. Leathery blue leaves on purple stems that sprawl or climb (to 5 feet) support white, 8-inch trumpet-shape flowers that unfurl at twilight, releasing an exotic perfume, only to wither in the cruel morning sun. All parts are poisonous. Mulch its growing places generously in winter. This is an exception to my usual prejudice against imported exotica.

Eupatorium coelestinum   Hardy Ageratum

Wonderful, 2-foot or more fall bloomer, in sun or partial shade. Blue flower clusters. I use this invasive perennial as an annual planted in containers, where it is spectacular.

Gaillardia pulchella   Blanket Flower

3-foot sun-loving bushy North American native with double flowers in gaudy oranges, reds, and yellows for which one is usually grateful in August when others have spent themselves.

Gypsophila elegans   Baby's Breath

Clouds of tiny, white flowers on a bushy 2-foot plant. Good for
transitions or background role. The perennial achillea 'The Pearl'
performs the same task and is more summer hardy. Needs sun.

Helianthus   Sunflower

Natives of North America—3–10 feet tall, single and double
forms, mostly yellow, disease-free background plants for full sun.
Let the birds graze on the huge seedpods all winter long. Why not
cultivate a whole field of sunflowers?

Heliotropium arborescens   Heliotrope

Old-fashioned, 18-inch high handsome plant, for sun or partial
shade, with deep violet-blue flower clusters, beautiful veined dark-
green leaves. Excellent container plant though more thirsty than
most. Worth wintering over in a cool greenhouse.

Impatiens

Everyone should promise not to clutter suburbia with one more
half whiskey barrel (near the mailbox) of this happy, self-reliant,
continuous-blooming plant (usually no more than 2 feet high). But
is there a better plant for hanging baskets and shade decoration?
Drought resistant and trouble-free in many agreeable colors and
varieties—of course it is the most overused plant in the world, doing
the job with absolutely no temperament. Encourage it with a weekly
feeding of diluted all-purpose plant food and keep out of the way.

Ipomoea purpurea   Morning Glory

The cultivar 'Heavenly Blue' is my favorite climbing and trailing
annual, a vine growing up to 10 feet. We send it up arches, walls
and fences for spectacular airborne displays. This plant is a natural
strangler. Plant it with the night-blooming white moonflower—
another *Ipomoea* twiner and twister—and let them have at it.

Lathyrus odoratus   Sweet Pea

Everyone's grandmother grew this lovely, delicate, romantic, demanding little vine. Start from seed in containers, hanging baskets, and under trellises. Needs constant pinching back and deadheading to produce summerlong blooms.

Lobularia maritima   Sweet Alyssum

Spreading mats of tiny white or purple flowers 3 to 6 inches high for containers or gardens. This plant never tires of blooming and requires no maintenance—just well-drained soil. Loves to crawl around between paving stones and bricks where it might even reseed itself.

Nicotiana   Flowering Tobacco

Nicotiana sylvestris of the soaring spikes up to 4 feet and tubular white flowers is a better performer than the touted 'Niki' hybrids, which crumples in the noonday sun and attracts whiteflies. Reseeds itself nicely—just be careful in spring weeding, but that should be second nature by now.

Papaver   Poppy

Iceland, Shirley, and California poppies—to have flowers such as these is the reason why people garden. Sow the seeds in three-week intervals during early spring to enjoy their delicate and fragile pale-colored blooms on 2–4-foot stalks most of the summer. Let them reseed or collect and dry the seedpods for the following year's crop.

Pelargonium   Geranium

The same genus as the scented geranium (page 111). I suppose because they submit to neglect and never actually die, ivy-leafed geraniums (*P. peltatum*) and the mixed hybrids are favorite summer annuals all over the United States and Europe. They can grow to 3 feet, but most are half that size. They require constant deadheading and trimming to make them look halfway decent and to control their rangy growing habits. I always try a few and realize once again that I like plants that need less grooming a lot better.

Tagetes patula   Marigold

French dwarf marigolds up to 10 inches high allegedly deter insects and are nice low-growing, well-behaved yellow-and-orange flowered plants that many gardeners simply hate. I like them mixed in with herbs, and I believe insects and animals don't like them any more than people do.

Tropaeolum   Nasturtium

'Dwarf Jewel' series, a foot high, planted around herbs is a classic garden scenario. The climbing (up to 6 feet) or trailing variety attracts hummingbirds and will bolt over walls and fences with astonishing speed. Nasturtiums dislike disruption—sow seeds in peat pots after an overnight soak in water to hasten germination.

Viola   Pansy

The same genus as Johnny-jump-up (page 113), but larger—6–12 inches. Partial to light shade. For window boxes, tubs, pots, and gardens, everyone's favorite spring plant. Deadhead for continuous bloom. In June overplant with impatiens—pansies fade away in summer heat.

Zinnia elegans

Showy midsummer blooms in many varieties, colors, sizes, and shapes, but in some gardens zinnias are not truly garden worthy as the foliage is fungus-prone and turns shabby. A good cutting-garden flower where a little mildew doesn't matter. Aren't baskets of cut zinnias the essence of summer?

Some Alien
Annuals

gladiolus

*F*lamboyant, brilliant, showy, fiery, rich, intense, glossy, radiant, immense, sparkling, dazzling, show-stopping, and flashy are a few of the encomiums that plant and seed merchants squander on the annuals in the following list. To insert these tropical oddballs, with their curious blooms and bizarre foliage patterns, into our northern gardens, with the understated sophistication of our own native plants, invites botanical disunity and disarray. Flamboyant tropical plants with their arriviste posture are suitable for southern gardens under palm and bougainvillea, for nesting birds of paradise, or for amusing toddlers in public parks. Plants that are more environmentally compatible deserve our focus: They are better-looking and better behaved, and don't scream for attention.

Amaranthus tricolor   Joseph's Coat

Summer poinsettia with chocolate, orange, and red leaves; 4-foot tropical accent plant, beloved of bedding-out designers.

Caladium hortulanum

Nonhardy tubers with off-the-wall leaf designs, inspirational to wallpaper manufacturers in the 1930s.

Canna

Tuberous giant with massive blooms in disharmonious colors; simply inadmissible.

Celosia cristata   Cockscomb

Lamentable colors with uncomely plumes or brain-shaped flower heads; ugh!

Coleus

Another varicolored foliage plant with striped and splashed designs on ruffle-edged leaves, painted in chocolate, scarlet, yellow, salmon, mahogany, and chartreuse.

Gladiolus x *hortulans*

All-American sickroom flower.

Salvia splendens   Scarlet Salvia

Fiery scarlet florets on spikes, exploited by park gardeners across the globe. It is important to find other solutions for the red problem.

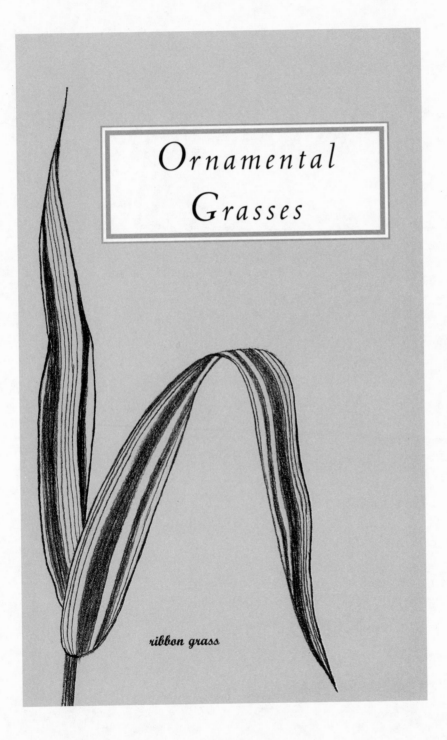

Ornamental Grasses

ribbon grass

One venerable British gardener-author opines that ornamental grass gardens "make an eccentric statement." Bah and humbug! For a growing number of American gardeners, ornamental grass gardens make the consummate horticultural statement, an ever-changing spectacular of textures and colors: towering stalks capped with snow, swaying in winds, bladed leaves glistening in the rain, colors changing from summer blues and greens to coppery bronze autumn shades and finally the dried wheat hues of winter. If such a garden is eccentric, then so be it.

Most of the grasses that have acclimated so naturally in American gardens are natives of Asian tundras and, it is rumored, don't do for the Brits, neither flowering nor changing colors as the season advances. Moreover, grasses are not widely available in British garden centers and must be ordered from specialist nurseries.

Our island grass garden is the focal point in the front of our property. It stands before a grove of dark hemlocks whose inner depths turn black under the summer sun. We composed this garden with an assembly of various miscanthus giants, fountain grasses with two- to seven-foot spreads, Japanese blood grass, blue oat grass, and the striped ribbon grasses. This collection of just a few grasses is endlessly fascinating to us and to the birds, winter and summer.

We also plant grasses in our mixed border gardens to give weight and texture and to solve problems. The fountain grasses will grow in places where nothing else seems to work.

The grass garden is mined with daffodil bulbs, which flower in early spring. The new blades of grass camouflage the dying bulb foliage. While grasses solicit and welcome the company of compatible summer-flowering natives such as rudbeckia, coreopsis, and helianthus, we have resisted the temptation so far, though we do allow the two large clumps of Queen-Anne's-lace, which just dropped in, to assert the rights of domicile.

The big grasses conceal neighbors, roads, and buildings. They soften walls, fences, and pavements. A few are shade tolerant, but most prefer sun, excellent drainage, and rich loamy soil. They require little maintenance other than a spring shearing and about six inches of mulch to control weeds and retain moisture. We stake the sixteen-foot stalks of miscanthus in early summer to guard against bashing by summer rains and winds. New plants must be well watered until they are established.

Start with any of the plants in the following list, their varieties and cultivars. Use them in mixed borders, as landscape accents, or in their own highly visible space. They may be eccentric, but they put on a sensational spring, summer, autumn, and winter performance demanding little in return.

Carex morrowii 'Aurea Variegata'   Grass

Clump-forming, 1–2 feet high, yellow and green swirling grass-like blades. While not a true grass, it makes a good border and edging plant in sun or partial shade.

Festuca ovina var. Glauca   Blue Fescue

Dense mounds of silver-blue blades 6–12 inches long, often used as a ground cover or in groups as an accent plant. Full sun.

Hakonechloa macra 'Aureola'

Trendy Japanese import with yellow-and-green striped leaves 6–18 inches long and inconspicuous flowers. Decorative, unusual, slow, and low grower in full or partial shade.

Helictotrichon sempervirens   Blue Oat Grass

Blue leaf blades, 2-foot clumps with high floating panicles. Superb plant for mixed borders, as an accent or in groups.

Imperata cylindrica 'Rubra'   Japanese Blood Grass

Another recent Japanese import with plenty of cachet. Brilliant, slender, red blades form 2-foot clumps. Plant in groups to make a noticeable statement in partial shade. Slow grower.

Miscanthus

These are giant members of the grass family and range in clumps from 4–16 feet of stalks and blades. They are dramatic, strong plants, not suitable for most mixed borders, but rather as accents around ponds and streams, screening and background or as the star players with other ornamental grasses in their own garden. The best advice is to make several research expeditions to your local plant emporiums to see what is available. Chinese silver grass and the variegated porcupine and zebra grasses are our favorites.

Pennisetum   Fountain Grass

These are the fountain grasses ranging from 1–6 feet of gracefully arching blades with silvery brown panicles blooming in late August. They are beautiful, versatile, and dramatic plants, winter and summer, and wonderful problem solvers in mixed borders as accent plants or in company with other species of the *Pennisetum* and *Miscanthus* genera. Investigate and experiment with all sizes and colors in various situations.

Phalaris arundinacea var. 'Picta'   Ribbon Grass

Green-and-white striped blades forming 2- to 4-foot spreading clumps in sun or shade. Extremely aggressive but worth the effort to control it; or plant it in bottomless containers to prevent spreading. Cut back in midsummer to encourage fresh new blades. This plant, so light in color and with such graceful blades, is a good choice for difficult and shady places where it can have its invasive way.

The Vertical Vines

clematis jackmanii

*I*n painting on a two-dimensional surface, painters exploit the tensions created between rising and falling movements—the vertical axes that activate pictorial space and are in opposition to horizontal movement. These tensions or polarities created with lines or volumes lend mystery and power to paintings by avoiding stasis, a static situation of balance where all appears to be of equal weight and on the same level. Artists control space by establishing dynamic thrusts with vertical, horizontal, and tilted axes. In the garden we can do no less and much more because our stage is three-dimensional. We have the dimension of depth as well as the vertical and horizontal dimensions to organize on our garden stage.

Until recently I had overlooked the importance of the vertical dimension. Now, however, our gardens are off the ground literally and figuratively because of the visual interest created by rising or climbing vines and those that trail and unwind from hanging baskets.

We give the "Best Climber" award to our two glorious sweet autumn clematis, overreaching clumps of white star-shaped fragrant blossoms in late summer, covering corners of the house around the back gardens. Another favorite is the honeysuckle 'Red Trumpet', a container-grown woody vine, supported by lattice attached to a wall of the house around the kitchen herb garden. Its season-long, deep-scarlet, trumpet-shaped blossoms entice hummingbirds and bees. 'Red Trumpet' thrives as few others will, in the intense heat of this particular microclimate.

Nearby, several clematis *C. x jackmanii* and *C.* 'Nelly Moser' along with morning glories and climbing nasturtiums scale the tall lattice fence enclosing this herb garden, their upward motion emphasized by the downward thrust of sweet pea wands trailing from hanging baskets. In one of our mixed border gardens, the 'White Dawn' rose and clematis *C. x jackmanii* and *C. montana* climb lattice supports attached to the house, blooming intermittently most of the summer.

In the back herb garden, I picture the clematis 'Duchess of Edinburgh' and morning glories 'Heavenly Blue' climbing and twining together around a black steel trellis arch. Alas, the lackluster appearance of the Duchess (from mail-order bare root stock origin) makes for an annual nonevent, and 'Heavenly Blue' carries the scene alone. This duchess gets one more chance, before being replaced by a less diffident member of her family, such as *C. montana*, a plant that couldn't care less where and with what it consorts.

Another superb clinger and climber is *Hydrangea petiolaris*, which we train to grow horizontally over a low brick wall, more for its sturdy shiny green leaves than its short-lived white flower clusters.

I list the following few reliable vines; they are easy to grow, require little maintenance, and are notably decorative. Assign them to walls, fences, trellises, lattice, and trees to give your garden the vertical extension and a delightful airborne flower show.

There are some vines out there that garden books and nurseries purvey with a total lack of horticultural or civic responsibility. One is bindweed and the other is bittersweet. Their roots are entangled deep in the underworld and issue forth where they please—a gardener's nightmare. Take sound advice and steer clear of these plant kingdom hooligans and excise them on sight, should they discover your property. Another caution is the trumpet vine (*Campsis radicans*), which will decorate an outbuilding or fence in no time with beautiful scarlet trumpetlike flowers. However, its wandering roots observe no restrictions and can emerge in the most unlikely places.

Clematis

There are at least 300 types of the glamorous and notoriously difficult clematis. Many gardeners are put off by their mysterious behavior and demanding, confusing requirements, seldom explained with cogency by growers and dealers. The pruning thing is of the utmost importance in clematis culture, and instructions on pruning, when and how, should be attached to every plant that is sold. Some clematis bloom on the previous year's wood and are pruned only after flowering, while others bloom on the current year's growth and can be pruned to within three feet of the ground in early spring. The horticultural mysteries increase when a happy-looking specimen one day wilts and perishes the next, as you watch. Wilt rot! One is advised to consult a plant pathologist and administer a biweekly dose of fungicide spray. My advice is to dismiss any plant demanding such ridiculous attentions and grow something else.

No matter, a garden is not a garden without these beauties. Give them the best start by preparing a planting hole composed of the best-textured light, loamy, alkaline soil. Shade their roots with a leafy annual. Heavy leaf or bark mulch can trigger the dreaded clematis wilt. Keep the moisture level even: not too wet, not too dry. With luck your reward could be the spectacle of these delightful flowering vines rambling over posts, fences, trellises, and walls in a never-ending succession of blooms.

While I intend to experiment with some of the hundreds of other types, these listed below have done well in our gardens, fairly undemanding and disease resistant.

Clematis maximowicziana   Sweet Autumn Clematis

Formerly known as *C. paniculata*, this one just grows and grows. Give it plenty of space to do its thing and stand back for its spectacular autumn exhibition. Disease-free; cut back to 2 feet in late autumn.

Clematis x *jackmanii*

Well-behaved, 12-foot climber with violet-purple, 5-inch blooms from early summer to September in sun or partial shade. Prune back in early spring.

Clematis montana   Anemone Clematis

This one is truly vigorous (up to 20 feet) and unpretentious. Our specimen grows over a water spigot, climbs a drainpipe, hits the gutter, and keeps on moving. This summer it may cover the roof. I wouldn't dream of thwarting its ambitions, though experts advise an after-blooming thin-out. The blooms are small, pink or white.

Clematis 'Nelly Moser'

Old reliable fast-climbing favorite, with pale mauve and pink blossoms in May and June and possibly September. Prune sparingly in early spring; flowers appear on current year's growth.

Hydrangea anomala petiolaris   Climbing Hydrangea

June-blooming clinger, perfect for stone or brick walls. Large flat flower heads, lustrous green leaves, and disease-free. Requires guidance but little pruning.

Lonicera sempervirens   Trumpet Honeysuckle

Handsome, hardy, and disease-free, with orange to scarlet trumpet-shaped flowers, in partial shade or blazing sun. Excellent container-grown plant but needs lattice support. Prune back to 10 inches in late fall.

Parthenocissus quinquefolia   Virginia Creeper

Such a big name for this woodland creeper! Though it is invasive there are places where it does a fine job of keeping out unwanted plants and demands little in return. The leaves turn brilliant scarlet in autumn. We encourage them to climb over our stone walls along the borders and to ascend certain trees but to keep a decent distance, or else. And, of course, you know about Boston ivy, an uptown cousin more suitable for elegant and highly visible places.

Rosa 'White Dawn'   Climbing Rose

Good foliage, double white flowers, trellis scaler. 'New Dawn', another cultivar, comes in pink. Remove aging canes every spring and mound roots with a foot of earth mulch for winter protection. This rose, the relatively carefree 'Bonica', and a few David Austins are the only roses that we grew as they resist black spot, rust, fungus, and Japanese beetles, all problems that require constant chemical or organic control.

Small Shrubs— Plants That Add Weight and Form to Mixed Borders

cone flower seedpod

*S*ubshrubs are undershrubs or small shrubs that may have partially herbaceous stems and are wonderful to use in composing mixed borders. Gardeners depend on them for a long and reliable performance throughout the growing season. Listed below are a few plants to consider that add weight, form, and decorative flowers to mixed border gardens with interesting season-long foliage colors and textures. They are relatively maintenance-free except for spring pruning and shaping and are available in most garden centers. Further, they are a hardy, fairly disease-resistant and self-reliant bunch, content in normal, well-prepared soil.

Buddleia davidii   Butterfly Bush

> 12 to 15 feet high. Sun. There are many vari-
> eties of *B. davidii* (or its hybrids) and their pur-
> plish or white flowers borne on spraying
> branches lure butterflies. Cut back almost to
> the base each spring.

Berberis thunbergii 'Crimson Pygmy'   Japanese Barberry

> This 2-foot shrub is of special merit because
> of its wonderful dense purple-maroon foliage,
> which is so appealing near golden-leafed
> plants. Sun or shade.

Caryopteris **x** *clandonensis*   Blue Spirea

Beautiful gray foliage with late-blooming sprays up to 5 feet of delicate blue flowers. Makes a stunning border along a wall or fence. Sun lover. Cut way back in spring.

Daphne

Many cultivars to choose from, but the most au courant and coveted is the hard-to-find, virus-prone 'Carol Macke', a lovely mounding 3–4-foot bush with variegated green and white leaves and fragrant white spring blossoms. *D.* x *burkwoodii* has been around longer and has a less iffy reputation. Sun or shade.

Graminae (grasses) See "Ornamental Grasses," pp. 129–134.

Hydrangea

So many species and cultivars of this no-maintenance, popular, problem-free genus, happy in sun or shade. Investigate—especially *H. macrophylla* and *H. villosa.* 5–8 feet. Some cultivars need cutting back in spring or fall. Sun.

Hypericum patulum 'Hidcote'

Stunning bright-yellow saucerlike flowers in late June with dark shiny green leaves on spraying branches. 2–3 feet, most happy in a sunny place. Cut back in early spring.

Juniperus   Juniper
Picea   Spruce

Both of these coniferous shrubs, growing in pyramidal or columnar shapes from 2–10 feet in sun or shade, make strong vertical accents and add authority and drama to the garden in summer and winter. There are many cultivars, colors, and textures to consider. Think of planting them in wooden tubs or barrels.

Potentilla Cinquefoil

A nice family of summer-flowering shrubs up to 4 feet to use as a hedge or planted singly. These are rugged, hardy plants, disease- and insect-free, and need little attention. Give them sun in good soils and they will perform for years. There are many varieties with small yellow, white, or pink blooms. Prune and thin in early spring.

Rosa 'Bonica' Shrub Rose

Ever-blooming, sun-loving, shrublike bush up to 6 feet or more needing less maintenance than the hybrids. Cut back in spring, mound with earth in the winter to protect crown. In October one finally tires of their incessant little clusters of pink blooms.

Spiraea Spirea

One hears that discerning gardeners will not grow these disease- and insect-free, fast-growing shrubs in valuable garden space—their loss. *S.* x *bumalda* is well worth the space and the effort for its pretty, long-lasting pink blooms on a dense 2-foot high bush.

Bulbs

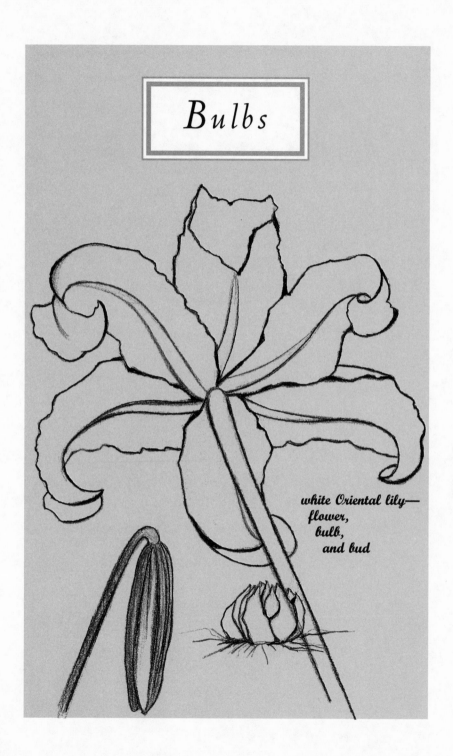

white Oriental lily—
flower,
bulb,
and bud

*C*olonies of daffodils, scillas, and crocus have settled in here and naturalized under trees and shrubs, around rocks, and along walls and fences. There was a time when we buried the tiny bulbs of *Iris reticulata*, fritillaria, crocus, and hyacinths in our gardens, but only a few crocus have survived the constant upheavals in these beds. Planting more seems fruitless. I love (and who doesn't?) the springtime show-garden spectaculars of beds of single-colored tulips, but they are not for the keepers of small gardens even to think of trying. Consider the labor of lifting and storing the bulbs after bloom and replanting the spaces with annuals or, worse, the two-and-a-half-month spectacle of desiccating tulip foliage. Moreover, in our region unless one gardens between barbed-wire fences, tulips are deer food.

Naturalized daffodils around the borders escort our gardens into early summer and then depart, leaving their places to the wandering volunteers, perilla, feverfew, ferns, and, well . . . weeds. We always plan to plant hundreds of bulbs every fall—there is no such thing as too many daffodils. As the foliage must die back naturally, a period that lasts into early summer while the bulb stores food for next year's performance, daffodils are a bit messy for mixed borders unless camouflaged by large-leafed plants. Some gardeners strangle the foliage in fussy little knots, but that is the sort of useless, boring chore to avoid. Besides, it's bad for the plant.

Lilium   Lily

Lilies from the great hybrid groups—Asiatic, Aurelian, Tiger, and Oriental—are the garden superstars all summer long with cultivar names as beguiling as their faces: 'Red Night,' 'Connecticut King,' 'Pink Perfection,' 'African Queen,' 'Brush Stroke,' 'Silly Girl,' 'Raspberry Fizz,' 'Tiger Babies,' and more. Hybridizers have produced hundreds of species with blossoms of so many shapes: trumpet, chalice, pendant, bowl, sunburst, and so-called reflexed, with colors ranging from dawn blushes to brilliant sunny oranges and reds. They are all irresistible. Choice is tantalizing, decision making excruciating, and we always find the space to sponsor a few more varieties. Some like shade, some like it hot. They take up little room, require little maintenance, are a cinch to grow, and are good mixers—a class act with other perennials—and naturalize effortlessly in semishade borders, especially with ferns. The North American Lily Society recommends buying American-grown bulbs, as foreign imports may be less than fresh and are sometimes waxed and rootless. Lilies need their little roots.

We started our own lily collection with a grower's choice that included all of the hybrids just noted, and we add a few more species of lilies every year. They are my favorite horticultural model, holding their pose very nicely for several days, and submit to spending lonely nights in an old icebox to prolong their life span.

Bulbs arrive in plastic bags, protected with slightly damp peat moss. Be sure to order precooled bulbs and follow planting instructions. Generally, we plant bulbs in groups of 3, in rich humus soil,

16 inches apart and 4–6 inches deep, behind shorter, leafier plants for shade and to cover their stems after flowering. Stems must be left to a natural demise. After fertilizing, we water and mulch with small pine bark chips. We fertilize again in early spring. Never use manure near lilies; it harbors unfriendly organisms that may trigger the viruses and fungi to which they are prone.

Good drainage and air circulation are absolutely essential to the well-being and prosperity of lilies. Pick faded flowers, pods, and petals after bloom. Remove old stems and debris in the fall. Mulch generously with salt hay after the ground freezes. Such preventive measures seem to keep our lilies disease-free and are more environmentally sound than the ten-day spray regime with chemicals that *they* advise lily and rose fanciers to undertake. If a lily is troubled, out it goes and into the garbage. (Never put diseased garden debris in the compost.)

Lilies adapt to growing up in containers. Given their long-lasting blooms, it is well worth the effort to plant a few pre-cooled bulbs in 6-inch plastic pots filled with a light commercial potting soil over some pebbles to ensure good drainage. Keep the soil moist (not soggy), place in good light with temperatures around 60 degrees. Fertilize with an all-purpose liquid fertilizer every two weeks. In two and a half months or so, they will be ready, pots and all, to go into a larger basket or terra-cotta container and be moved to the center of attention. After blooming replant the lilies (stem and bulb) in the garden. Whatever, don't even think of gardening without hybrid lilies—the perfect flower.

Narcissus   Daffodil, Jonquil

The *Narcissus* genus is divided into eleven main divisions and eighteen subdivisions. There are hundreds of cultivars, and new ones are introduced every year. We experiment and take our chances with bulbs ordered from catalogues. Pricey bulbs go in prominent places, and the less dear ones are sent out to naturalize and form colonies.

It is easy to succumb to the enticing verbal and photographic visions in the bulb catalogues; short and frilly, tall and aloof, early and late blooming, wind and weather resistant, double- and single-blossomed, and those of delicate fragrance. They come in ice-cream colors—lime, peach, apricot, gold, lemon, cream, and white—and many bear awards of merit from distinguished horticultural societies. Call a friend who has moved to Florida and ask what spring is like without daffodils and then order hundreds more than you had planned.

Plant daffodil bulbs in good soil, about 4–5 inches deep and 6–8 inches apart in groups of twelve or more in each planting hole. Massings and informal groupings are preferable to planting in straight lines and regular spacing. Roots have more time to become established if bulbs are planted in early fall, though November is not too late. Fertilize after planting with a bulb-specific compound and again in early spring. Water immediately. Do not cut off leaves until they turn yellow in early summer.

Scilla hispanica (Hyacinthoides hispanicus)   Squill

This Spanish native is the showiest of the scillas, with tall, slender, 20-inch stems and little hanging azure blue bells. Scillas are happy naturalizers in light or deep shade and loamy soil. I dig up some of the little bulbs now and then to start new colonies. Unlike daffodils and tulips, scillas couldn't care less about having their tall arching bladelike leaves cut to the ground shortly after their long blooming period. We replant their spaces with the shallow-rooted impatiens.

Tulipa   Tulip

Since the mid-seventeenth century when Holland went berserk over tulips and speculation caused a single bulb to fetch thousands of dollars, prices have dropped considerably. For a few pennies we have a choice from hundreds of cultivars. However, economic sanity begets new problems: decision making and the will to resist ordering the store. Alas, our own gardens are bereft of this elegant flower (one of my favorite subjects to draw and paint) since our neighborhood gang of deer decapitated a handsome stand of full-blooming species tulips in one dreadful foray.

Planting tulips requires a sensible and philosophic attitude, for if marauding deer don't eat them rodents, insects, and other pests are standing in line for the kill. And there are other mysterious events that cause tulips to dematerialize or fail to bloom. Lucky gardeners—the ones without deer—regard tulips as annuals. They plant them in clumps and drifts behind large-leafed plants and simply expect a little natural attrition.

We do jam a few half whiskey barrels near the house with our tulips-of-the-year choices and also plant them in plastic growers' containers in the fall, to winter over in the compost pile. Wire netting protects the bulbs from predators. When they are about to bloom we bring them forth inside of willow baskets that fit over the growers' pots—a movable garden of the first spring flowers cultivated without anxiety.

Ground Covers and Underplants

European wild ginger

G round covers, the living mulch, keep the soil cool and moist, discourage weeds, and control erosion as they wander around between plants, decorating and filling vacuums in shade or sun gardens. They are a stout lot, undaunted by difficult assignments and requiring little maintenance. Give them spaces in your garden to weave together in a low-growing tapestry of varied foliage and pretty little blooms. Send them out to cover where others refuse to grow, reminding them occasionally not to exceed their boundaries.

The following list includes some of the useful and decorative ground covers, easily available from the gardens of friends or commercial suppliers.

Chrysanthemum pacificum (Ajanja pacificea)

Silver-edged foliage plant, elegant, ornamental, and hardy—the new darling of the plant world, discovered lollygagging around in Japan a mere ten years ago. Deserves prime space, favors sun, forms 12-inch or more mounds of variegated foliage, with tiny yellow blooms just before frost. Cut back in spring.

Dianthus   Carnation, Pink

A popular old-fashioned plant with confusing nomenclature, a result of promiscuous interbreeding and confused parentage. Nevermind, there are many strains of this disease- and pest-free plant with which to design a low-growing tapestry around borders or under taller companions. They are low, mat-forming and mounding, in shades of pink, white, and red, and prefer sun and good soil with fast drainage. Shear occasionally to renew vigor.

Epimedium x *versicolor* 'Sulphureum'   Barrenwort

Good for mulching under shrubs or other difficult places. Pretty reddish-green leaves and insignificant little yellow blossoms. Durable and quick spreader in partial sun and partial shade.

Geranium   Cranesbill

Hardy geraniums, not to be confused with the global pot favorites and bedding plants, which are known as geraniums but are, in fact, of the genus *Pelargonium* (see pages 122–123). There are many species and cultivars of this easy-to-grow, disease- and pest-resistant, long-flowering, spreading, mounding, sun or shade garden winner. Some are dwarf and prostrate, producing mats of foliage and flowers. Shearing encourages new blooms.

Hedera helix   English Ivy

There are many varieties of hardy ivy to do drudge work in difficult places: to trail, climb, hang, and cling. It is evergreen, easy to grow, and useful, even ornamental under shrubs and along banks and sloping ground. Not appropriate for proper garden spaces.

Juniperus horizontalis   Creeping Juniper

A valuable and ornamental prostrate shrub of blue-green foliage, useful for erosion control, around rock gardens, or with other ornamental shrubs. *Juniperus horizontalis* and *J. communis* deserve mention, which may not be helpful, as growers and specialists are involved in a protracted nomenclature squabble. This is the unusual plant that thrives in hot, poor soil, even sand dunes, and in cool acid soil as well.

Pachysandra terminalis   Japanese Spurge

Arguably, a certified bore with only one objective: self-multiplication ad infinitum across suburban landscapes. The chances of finding older properties without mother lodes of the stuff are improbable, as in the old days, after the depression and war years, homeowners had fewer choices and considerably less interest in gardening than we do today. Ergo, pachysandra, which is evergreen and easy to grow, was a face-saving solution. At least one was making an effort. Our gratitude to the former owners of our place is deep indeed for the groves of pachysandra that cover the gray areas, where we have neither the time nor interest to garden. Pachysandra bashing is futile. Let it work for you—spread itself mindlessly in spaces that even weeds eschew, serve as mulch under shrubs, and control erosion. But send it packing if it sneaks into prime garden spaces reserved for more decorous and decorative underplanting.

Phlox subulata   Moss Pink

Hardy border edger about 6 inches high, bearing profuse spring blooms in lavender, pink, or white. Needs full sun with good drainage to encourage well-behaved wandering.

Vinca minor   Periwinkle

A nice-looking, trailing vinelike ground cover, with little blue blossoms. Useful cover for beds of spring bulbs or under foundation planting, but not distinguished enough for more prestigious spaces.

The following ground covers are more delicate and less utilitarian than the plants just mentioned. They are the ones known as greeters and drifters, weaving and unifying with their delicate foliage and pretty blooms.

Ajuga pyamidalis   Bugle Weed

Asarum europaeum   European Wild Ginger

Astilbe chinensis 'Pumila'

Galium odoratum   Sweet Woodruff

Lamium   Spotted Nettle

Pulmonaria officinalis   Common Lungwort

Thymus   Thyme

Astilbe is described in "Composing with Perennials," pp. 93–100. All other ground covers in this list are described in "Composing with Herbs," pp. 103–113.

Shade and Wildflower Gardens

jack-in-the-pulpit

*S*hade gardens are sites for the understated and modest members of the plant kingdom; self-effacing, undemanding plants that generate a canopy of varied foliage and blooms from spring until frost.

Our shade gardens wander along the back stone wall borders of our property and decorate several other spaces closer to the house. Many of our plants are memories of bygone gardens here that we rescued from the old compost piles: bleeding hearts, jack-in-the-pulpits, columbines, foxgloves, monkshood, and scilla. In other fertile hunting grounds along unkempt borders we found naturalized escapees: feverfew, ajuga, daisies, and tiger lilies. Horticultural archaeology.

Our shade gardens just sort of filled up with these wildings and we gave them some elegant and substantial companions—ferns, astilbes, and hostas—for weight, form, and structure.

The shade show begins in early spring with the blue bells of *Scilla hispanica* and collections of daffodils and wild blue phlox, planted behind hostas and ferns to shield their long and untidy demise. Forget-me-nots jump around at random with the other ground huggers: primrose, sweet woodruff, lamium, epimedium, ajuga, European wild ginger, and the kooky little Johnny-jump-ups. The shy woodland jack-in-the-pulpits, tamed by ferns, appear in self-perpetuating clusters along with big and little bleeding hearts and astilbes. The ferns arrive late and take their sweet time about uncoiling and spreading their arching fronds.

In June, purple and white foxgloves climb into pink and white laurel blossoms, flanked by columbines, bleeding hearts, and wild daisies. Bright and yellow, evening primrose lights the darkest places, and sweet cicely sweeps its fragrant airy foliage across its neighbors. Queen-Anne's-lace grows tall and willowy, and mulleins, the garden jesters, begin their vertical thrust.

In summer's deep shade, cimicifuga blooms on long bending wands and perilla and feverfew volunteers move into spaces vacated by spring's early arrivals. Japanese anemone's pink and white blossoms lean over hemerocallis and the aloof platycodons, with their prissy little white and blue blooms.

In September, cooler weather encourages the deep blue blossoms of monkshood to flower with the feathery plumes of goldenrod and the flaming red cork bushes: one of our garden's last spectaculars before frost.

These are just a few of the summer-long happenings in our shade gardens, which seem oblivious to heat, drought, pests, and humidity. Comparatively little maintenance is required other than a little regular grooming and spring and fall cleanup. We mulch with shredded cedar bark or small pine chips to keep plants clean and cool, and we spread a layer of salt hay for winter protection.

All plants need air and light. Most shade plants can tolerate filtered sun and, defying their reputation, often flourish in full sun. In some cases, double-digging is impossible because of tree roots, so prepare fertile humusy planting holes. Let ground covers with shallow roots wander over exposed tree roots and rocky soil.

Some wildflowers are available in nurseries and garden centers, but just be sure to ask if the stock has been propagated under simulated conditions and not removed from the wild. It is laudable for gardeners to rescue imperiled plants. Our wild geraniums, trillium, common hemerocallis, some ferns and *Phlox divaricata* once roamed the nearby roadsides and were doomed to extinction by bulldozer. I know from their proliferations here that they are grateful for our concern and intervention.

Shade gardens can really be the most rewarding gardens. The plants are self-reliant, well-groomed—not the least bit persnickety. I also think they are the most horticulturally interesting, often with outsized leaves and colors that deepen in the surrounding dark background. Rather than fret about shade, gardeners should exploit it for all of its potential: a place to make wonderful low-maintenance gardens that hold their own from early spring until late fall.

The following list includes shade plants growing in our gardens that are disease-free, drought tolerant, and winter hardy. Full descriptions of them may be found in other chapters of the book. So important are ferns and hostas that I give them pages of their own.

Perennials (see pages 93–100)

Anemone x hybrida   Japanese Anemone

Aquilegia   Columbine

Astilbe x arendsii

Campanula lactiflora   Milky Bellflower

Cimicifuga racemosa   Snakeroot

Dicentra spectabilis and *D. eximia*   Bleeding Heart

Hemerocallis   Daylily

Heuchera sanguinia   Coralbells

Hosta   Plantain Lily

Iris ensata   Japanese Iris

Iris sibirica   Siberian Iris

Kirengeshoma

Lilium   Lily

Oenothera tetragona   Evening Primrose

Phlox divaricata   Blue Phlox

Platycodon grandiflora   Balloonflower

Rodgersia

Herbs (see pages 103–113)

Aconitum carmichaelii   Monkshood

Ajuga pyramidalis   Bugle Weed

Asarum europaeum   European Wild Ginger

Chrysanthemum parthenium   Feverfew

Digitalis purpurea   Foxglove

Galium odoratum   Sweet Woodruff

Lamium   Spotted Nettle

Myosotis scorpioides   Forget-me-not

Myrrhis odorata   Sweet Cicely

Perilla frutescens

Pulmonaria officinalis   Common Lungwort

Viola tricolor   Johnny-jump-up

Subshrubs (see pages 143–148)

Berberis thunbergii 'Crimson Pygmy'   Japanese Barberry

Bulbs (see pages 149–156)

Narcissus   Daffodil, Jonquil

Scilla hispanica   Spanish Bluebell

Tulipa   Tulip

Ground Covers (see pages 157–162)

Epimedium x *versicolor* 'Sulphureum'   Barrenwort

Hedera helix   English Ivy

Pachysandra terminalis   Japanese Spurge

Vinca   Periwinkle

Hostas (see below)

Ferns (see page 171)

Wildflowers and Weeds (see pages 177–180)

Solidago   Goldenrod

Verbascum thapsus   Common Mullein

Hostas

In the last decade, hostas have come a long way horticulturally and have been mercifully released from those trite installations along driveways and walls. Now these showy, predictable, and dependable plants so refined of appearance and habit have assumed their rightful place in shade gardens—hegemony over all their botanical companions.

Hostas interbreed naturally and are interbred liberally by hybridizers. The consequence of all this promiscuity is an addled nomenclature for the more than 1,000 cultivars. Therefore, the best advice I have for hosta collectors is taking a straight path to local suppliers to see exactly what's new and what's what in hosta circles.

Your first choice might be the Brobdingnagian, slug-proof *H. sieboldiana* 'Elegans', five feet of spreading blue puckered leaves and fragrant white lilylike blossoms in midsummer. Plant it near the golden-leaved 'August Moon' and 'Frances Williams' of bluegreen-colored foliage with yellow borders. Spread before this trio a tapestry of low-growing Lilliputian hostas such as *H. venusta* or 'Tiny Tears'—their wee leaves and flowers diminished the more by comparison.

Hosta collecting comes naturally. One hosta calls for another and another. And why not? They are peerless, versatile, and without demands of any sort, other than a little stalk clipping after flowering. They seem to keep reinventing themselves with new color variations and size and shape of leaves.

While seldom requiring division, they tolerate the assault in early spring and heal themselves quickly. Slugs think some hosta leaves are yum-yum; therefore, water before noon, so the leaves and ground dry before nightfall. Keep the soil under hostas squeaky clean as slugs hide in debris and mulch. Slug compounds do deter these yucky creatures, but it's one more job to avoid, if possible. Hosta buffs have their own club, the American Hosta Society, where you can get information on the thousand or more cultivars, should you need to.

Ferns

Ferns have been around for millions of years, acquiring survival experience and know-how in wetlands, fields, alpine rocks, and dry shade. They are tolerant of difficult conditions in the wild as well as to domesticated suburban gardens. Give them a tough assignment, such as ground cover around overbearing shrubs or controlling erosion on sloping ground, and they will perform as few other plants can. Consider a fernery in deep shade composed with some of the elegant ferns surrounded by beautifully mulched spaces of small pine bark chips or shredded cedar bark and traversed by paths of large flat fieldstones.

Ferns are self-reliant and decorative. They send their graceful fronds to hide the weary, comfort the shy, and flatter their more accredited neighbors. They stick it out to the last, and the ostrich and cinnamon ferns turn to shades of brilliant gold as the nights grow colder.

One of the great pleasures of spring gardening is the daily review of the prehistoric-looking coils of cinnamon ferns unfurling into three feet of arching fronds.

I list below a few ferns that we plant in our gardens in various places with various shade-loving associates, especially hostas and jack-in-the-pulpits. We encourage the variegated green and white lamiums and sweet woodruff to wander around on the ground beneath them to form carpets of cooling mulch.

Adiantum pedatum   Maidenhair Fern

Elegant clump-forming ferns on skinny black stems with airy radiating fronds. Native.

Athyrium filix-femina   Lady Fern

Native spreader with little ego and willing to work hard to improve difficult places.

Athyrium niponicum (A. goeringianum) 'Pictum'   Japanese Painted Fern

The Japanese painted fern, with its two-foot curled fronds in variegated and muted grays, greens, and purples, is a desirable choice for the shade garden. Good growers and accept division gracefully, which is good because you can't have enough of these beauties.

Dennstaedtia punctilobula   Hay-scented Fern

Rapid spreader, invasive but serious ground cover for tough low-visibility places. Native.

Matteuccia pensylvanica   Ostrich Fern
Osmunda cinnamomea   Cinnamon Fern

Both the ostrich and cinnamon ferns, growing to 4–6 feet tall, are dramatic in groups with their spectacular, gracefully arching fronds. Plant them in shady, difficult places around corners of the house where nothing likes to grow or let them serve as background fill in a shade garden. Native.

Osmunda regalis spectabilis   Royal Fern

Native. Also growing up to 6 feet, this one is considered the most elegant of all ferns. It is also aloof and diffident about the company it keeps so just move it around until it's happy.

Polystichum acrostichoides   Christmas Fern

Evergreen, with 2-foot fronds; a decorative and useful plant, it's happy wherever it resides. Cut back in early spring and divide every few years. Native.

Wildflowers or Weeds?

detail of
mullein stalk,
early summer

*E*very region has its distinctive flora—wildflowers which may be native plants or introduced plants. In this book, native refers to those plants indigenous to northeast North America or to a neighboring region. Other plants grow in such great abundance along roadsides, abandoned fields, and sometimes in our gardens that they are thought to be native but are in fact alien or exotic, meaning not part of our native flora. Over time plants from other countries have intentionally or unintentionally been brought into our country and have naturalized in fields and woods, mingling and competing with our native flora. A weed is a plant growing where it is not wanted; therefore, any plant can be a weed.

In our gardens many of my favorite plants also grow in the fields and woods around our property, where they have long since gone bush. I do not think they are wretched, unattractive, or useless, even though they may be officially classified as weeds. Plant snobs sniff at the sight of field and roadside plants enjoying such a la-di-da position here, but then this is no proper garden. Proper gardens are informed by English-style gardens and inhabited by exotics and hybrids, imported and crossbred for splendid blooms, albeit often unreliable and undependable. Proper gardens and their keepers are not conned by wretched things from the horticultural underworld of weeds a.k.a. wildflowers.

We are not trying to re-create a primeval setting or anything like that, but these plants add much to the general spirit of our gardens. Their self-abandoned cloning habits insure humor and spontaneity as offspring emerge in unexpected places and combinations, covering for summer fugitives and dressing up dull spots. They come and go all season long, on their own agenda. Colonist housewives brought many of these plants here as a reminder of the Old World, which probably accounts for their cute folkloric names.

Yes, this is an informal approach and attitude to gardening and not for those who demand order on the garden floor. We weed and mulch the garden beds after the seedlings expose themselves near the middle of May, as the season's crop of wildflowers could be perceived as weeds. Knowing your plant leaves is a must, but it's high time for that anyhow. Sending strangers in to weed could be ruinous, for what do they know?

These are the American wildflowers/weeds that I encourage to grow and reseed in our gardens. If they get too weedy acting, visitors and converts are usually delighted to take some away.

❧ Bloodroot   An elusive native with white waxy flowers on a leafless stalk, blooming in early spring in deep foresty shade and humusy soil. Mark its spot as it disappears with the heat.

❧ Buttercup   A few appear here every year, and those little yellow blossoms bring back vague childhood memories of something. I cut them back in July when they get leggy.

❧ Butterfly weed   This wild one of the meadows with its soft orange flower clusters in midsummer gets high marks even from plant snobs for its irreproachable garden manners.

⌖ Cinquefoil   In spite of a perfectly awful reputation, our one and only wedged between two bricks is a neat, well-behaved plant with shiny palmate leaves and tiny yellow blossoms.

⌖ Daylilies   I mean the naturalized everyday ones that escaped early on from domestic comforts in favor of the roadside all over the Northeast. I count on them to fill in difficult peripheral situations where more sensitive plants fail from neglect.

⌖ Ferns   Lady, hay-scented, Christmas, ostrich, and cinnamon ferns all came from the gardens of friends or the roadside. We employ their graceful fronds in all of our shade gardens. See "Ferns," p. 171.

⌖ Pokeberry   In late June these elegant wildflowers/weeds arrive fully grown along the borders here, lurking behind important bushes, rather like sentinels. These plants grow to outrageous proportions, delighting some visitors. Others say, "But aren't these just roadside weeds?" I have done everything I can to encourage a return engagement next spring.

⌖ Queen-Anne's-lace   This European import has long since adapted itself to the nation's roadsides and fields and is one of my favorite garden flowers, flinging its pretty white blossoms about in midsummer when others with more elite credentials falter from the heat.

⌖ *Solidago*   Goldenrod   We let this roadside beauty loose along the back border. It is insignificant until late summer, when its gracefully branching and arching yellow flower clusters intermingle with deep-blue monkshood well into September.

⌖ Trillium   Delicate and elegant naturalizer and very North American. Likes light shade and rich soil. Mark its spot as it can't take the heat.

❧ *Verbascum*   Mullein   This common roadside biennial with its 12-foot stalks bearing tiny yellow flowers rising from a base of giant furry gray leaves loves to be invited into the best gardens. It asserts itself in the most prominent and unlikely places. Birds rest on its giant stalks and cast the seeds hither and yon, for next year's crop.

❧ Wild geranium   Tender, rather delicate and shy wild ones with fragile pink blossoms in early spring. I liberated several from a friend's garden, and their well-adjusted offspring thrive in shady low-visibility places.

I never buy wildflowers/weeds as friends, birds, and winds drop them here, and some just came with the place. As I have noted before, I rescue many from the roadsides where they are imperiled by chemicals and extinction by bulldozer. Environmental guardians frown on taking plants from fields and woodlands (unless they are about to be razed by real estate speculators), for that is how plants make the endangered species list.

Whenever you buy plants from mail-order houses or garden centers, it is important to make sure the stock was not removed from the wild but propagated under controlled conditions. Many native species are increasingly threatened with extinction by loss of habitat or woodland robbery by unscrupulous collectors. There are 3,000 endangered wildflowers in North America, and 400 are predicted to be extinct by the year 2000. As gardeners, we can help preserve our native plants by respecting their natural environment, questioning garden centers and growers about the origins of their stock, and establishing populations of rescued or nursery-propagated plants in our own gardens.

Some of My Favorite Plant Combinations

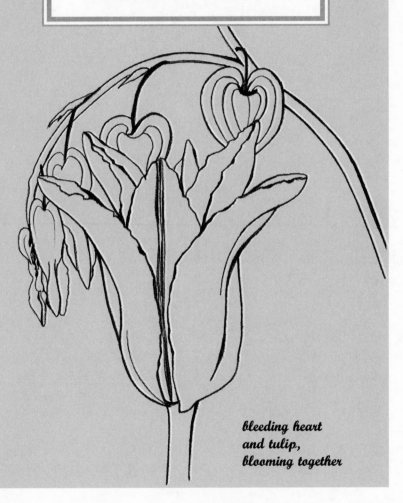

bleeding heart
and tulip,
blooming together

*I*n composing our gardens with the infinite combinations and assortments of perennials, small shrubs, herbs, vines, and ground covers, we preordain some of the horticultural happenings but depend on nature to arrange the unexpected events that give the gardens their natural-looking and unstudied appearance. We arrange certain plants that we know are just and meet together, but we depend on nature's wit to pose a clump of deep-purple Johnny-jump-ups in a grove of silvery gray lamb's ears, or to fling the wild geranium's pale-pink blossoms within the slender fronds of a cinnamon fern. Unplanned emergence appears all summer long in our gardens as various horticultural associations fuse, mingle, mix, and blend as they please. All gardens can be a stage for such limitless coincidence if their keepers encourage errant seedlings to have their way, at least some of the time.

With all those who write and speak about gardens, there is certainly no dearth of suggestions and advice on planting this with that. Nevertheless, here are some of my favorite combinations of flowering plants, listed according to their season of blooming. All plants are described in the plant lists and, I don't need to say yet once more, are regionally acclimatized to the Northeast.

❧ Let sweet woodruff's white blossoms mingle with the blue of forget-me-nots under hostas and ferns.

❧ Surround a grove of the elegant tall cinnamon or ostrich ferns with a ruffle of blue-blossomed Jacob's ladder.

❧ Permit the languid wands of bleeding heart, white or pink, to lean over an underplanting of 'Red Emperor' tulips—or any old tulip, for that matter.

❧ Encourage wild geraniums to consort with the tall elegant ferns or the big blue-leafed hostas.

❧ Help Johnny-jump-ups, pansies, and the lamium 'White Nancy' to establish interweaving colonies along shade borders.

❧ Set the ground cover *Ajuga pyramidalis* with its ten-inch purple stalks to wander around clumps of pinky-purple *Phlox subulata*.

❧ Plant groups of colorful pansies around maidenhair ferns, *Scilla hispanica*, and blue columbines.

❧ In a shady place order a constellation of the Japanese painted ferns with the delicate-stemmed maidenhair ferns and some broad-leafed chartreuse hostas.

Midsummer

❧ Throw the seeds of Iceland or Shirley poppies upon the snow in March around the 'Bonica' roses, foxgloves, lady's-mantle—anyplace.

✿ I love foxglove around a stand of Japanese or Siberian iris. They bloom simultaneously and the iris blades cover the demise of the foxglove. Foxgloves are gloriously showy under the pink and white blooms of our native laurel.

✿ Arrange for the golden-yellow swags of lady's-mantle, the gray foliage and delicate blue blossoms of nepeta, and meadow sage with its blue-lavender flower spikes to have their own position in a sunny garden.

✿ In partial shade let the yellow-blossomed, long-lasting evening primrose wander around between daylilies and ferns.

✿ Try planting baptisia with its delicate blue flowers on pale slender stalks near hemerocallis carrying pale-salmon or yellow blossoms on tall skinny stems.

✿ In the sun plant curly chives near liriope for a touching combination of low-down purple blossoms on little stems, blooming simultaneously in August.

✿ The exquisite orange flowers of asclepias, the butterfly weed, near the golden yellow flowers of the dwarf daylily, 'Stella d'oro', are just one more reason to convince this wild one to live in your garden.

✿ Along the back of a border, near the shiny-leaved, late-blooming monkshood, plant clumps of the thin-stalked five-footers: boltonia with its white daisylike flowers, physostegia with its pink and white clusters, and monarda with its white or fuchsia blooms.

✿ Give a collection of ornamental grasses some rudbeckia and helianthus for congenial August blooming company.

✿ In the sun, the Russian sage perovskia with its gorgeous blue-lavender flowers, near the blue daisylike flowers of *Aster frikartii* and the aggressively fertile annual cleome all do quite well together.

↝ Aruncus, the giant goatsbeard with its astilbe-like feathery flowers, and the equally tall spires of cimicifuga's fluffy white flowers perform aerial theatrics around the back of a shade garden in midsummer.

↝ The European wild ginger, asarum, with its low mounds of
round, shiny green leaves near the thin blades of the variegated liriopes
with their pale-lavender blooms, makes for a well-behaved and durable
ground-hugger for shady bowers.

Late Summer

↝ One of my favorite late-summer compositions combines the
plumes of goldenrod, the invader from the fields and woodlands, with
the purple blossoms of monkshood set before the flaming red of a
cork tree.

↝ The hardy blue ageratum *Eupatorium*, yellow chrysanthemums,
Sedum 'Autumn Joy', and the ferns turned golden keep things going very
nicely through September.

↝ Send the 'Sweet Autumn' clematis, with its white starlike flower-
lets, to clamber up posts and over roofs along with several 'Heavenly
Blue' morning glories for a late-summer show of strength.

↝ An assembly of monkshood, Japanese anemone with its long
wands bearing pink or white flowers, and the giant blue-leaved hosta,
sieboldiana 'Elegans' gives a garden a feeling of certitude. Try them
together.

For all of these considered incidents or fortunate accidents, most
flowers seem to coexist happily together without a lot of direction or
interference on my part. They harmonize in a sort of low-key, unself-

conscious manner without quarrel because, I am convinced, they are indigenous to this region and have grown accustomed to being together. Further, all the happy-go-lucky wandering volunteers keep everything changing from day to day, as they arrange and rearrange themselves into new and unexpected combinations with each other and the more significant perennials, demonstrating once more that the art of garden making is a deep and rich collaboration between nature and the gardener.

One Dozen Touted Plants Whose Performance Is Less Than Commendable and the Reasons Why

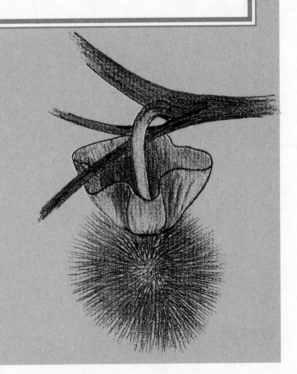

datura seed pod

*I*n the beginning we accepted with gratitude any plant that friends offered, so eager were we to get our gardens started. Some of my best friends donated several of the following plants, and others I actually bought and tried to grow, not realizing that some plants are dysfunctional in the Northeast's climate and soil, no matter how much you humor them.

I welcomed invasive plants and even encouraged them a bit. After all, anyone can discipline a plant, can't she? Eight years later I still pull out creeping jenny, goutweed, and yellow archangel tendrils as they sneak around in the garden.

Musk mallow, lythrum, and 'Alma Potschke', the aster, finally departed with little grace several years after they were actually thrown out. Lupine and delphinium broke my heart, making it very clear that our gardens would not do for the likes of them.

This list includes most of the plants that in our experience are without merit and some of the reasons why. Here they are, for what it's worth.

Aegopodium podagraria 'Variegata'   Goutweed

Swiftly creeping plant with beautiful white-edged leaves. Keep in solitary confinement between slabs of concrete.

Alcea rosea   Hollyhock

Don't be enticed by grandmother's garden favorite, which needs
staking, watering, deadheading, and, worse, is subject to homely
blight and rust.

Artemisia schmidtiana 'Silver Mound'

Low mounds of fine silky gray foliage that turns itself into a repre-
hensible, floppy mess by early summer. Cutting back solves the
problem, but why plant it in the first place? There are more hardy
silvery-gray plants, such as *Artemisia* 'Powis Castle'. (See "Composing with Herbs," pp. 103–113.)

Aster 'Alma Potschke'   Michaelmas Daisy

This four-foot overrated hybrid attracts whiteflies and mildew and
needs staking to hold up its branching stems, heavy with blooms
that are much too pink.

Centaurea cyanus   Cornflower

Long-stemmed, coarse-leaved flopping plant with so-so blue flowers
that turn unsightly and demand deadheading. One can do better.

Delphinium

The king of all flowers dislikes hot and humid summers. Even in
cooler areas it is susceptible to disease and pests such as slugs and
snails; needs staking, heavy feeding, and pruning. Sad but true. But
one has to find this out for oneself—at least three or four times.

Lamiastrum galeobdolon (*Galeobdolon luteum*)   Yellow Archangel

A terminator with global ambitions, sold as a nice ground cover
without warning labels to the unwary.

Lupinus   Lupine

Exquisite naturalizer in northern fields, but not easily coaxed to
perform with grace in domesticated circumstances.

Lysimachia nummularia   Creeping Jenny

Pretty spreading tendrils of shiny green leaves and darling little yellow flowers rooting itself every half inch to send forth more spreading tendrils—a nightmare scenario if it gets loose in the lawn. It always comes as a gift from someone.

Lythrum   Loosestrife

Tall spires of pink, purple, and rosy red flowers, hazardous to the environment and therefore outlawed in several states. A swamp and wetland clogger, sold widely without shame!

Malva moschata   Musk Mallow

Coarse five-footer, a rampantly self-sowing denizen of roadside and field, best left in situ to have its own aggressive way.

Papaver orientale   Oriental Poppy

Everyone's favorite spring bloomer in other people's gardens. Consummate transparent but short-lived blossoms on a rangy plant, leaving unattractive spaces during its long, slow, and messy demise. Many other plants are more garden-worthy though perhaps not quite as beautiful in their evanescence.

Gardening with Containers

my favorite Italian pot

The tradition of container gardening is part of the gardening heritage of the western world and is rooted in the ancient cultures of Egypt, Persia, Greece, and Rome. For thousands of years gardeners have used container plants to emphasize architectural rhythms and symmetries and create focal points in garden landscapes.

In Italy, where the memory of Roman, Pompeian, and Renaissance gardens still lingers, villagers line medieval streets or top garden walls with containers brimming over with brightly colored annuals and perennials. In formal villa gardens potted citrus trees often accent paths, walls, and spaces, just as they did in ancient gardens. And no Italian gardener lacks for pots of flowering geraniums and a tub of basil close to the kitchen.

Containers and pots are not only decorative and functional; they also bestow a romantic mood and spirit on any garden, regardless of its scale. A gardener's choice of containers, plants, and their placement is highly personal—depending on one's own artistic sensibilities.

My favorite container gardens are composed of stunning one-gallon olive oil cans, set on humble patios in rural Italian villages with their beautiful letters and designs showing through a tumble of splashy annuals. All pot gardeners collect pots obsessively and seek unusual but classical shapes and designs in terra-cotta, cast concrete, lead, and wood. (Plastic fake wood or terra-cotta look like plastic fake wood or terra-cotta.) There is no such thing as having enough pots or enough baskets. I love the rustic willow baskets and tuck them around filled with plants in their plastic growers' containers—easy to change, easy to move.

Terra-cotta accumulates a white film from salts and acids in fertilizers; this is acceptable. However, scummy algae looks disgusting, smothers roots, and attracts bacteria. An annual scrub—a little bleach and a lot of water—will keep pots clean. Before bringing in any tender plant for the winter, remove it from the pot to inspect it. Cut or scrape off any roots girdling the root ball. Wash the pot and repot the plant, using the same container if the proportions seem just. Potted perennials, herbs, and shrubs like spending the winter, unpotted, in the compost pile, protected and warm, or in a nursery bed mulched with salt hay after the ground freezes. Clean and store clay pots in a dry place or upside down in a protected place for the winter.

The secret of container gardening is that less is not more. In large pots, jam plants together with tall ones in the center surrounded by lower trailers and floppers such as morning glory, nasturtium, nicotiana, sweet peas, thyme, alyssum, and nepeta. Italian gardeners use several large, leafy, textured plants as a foil for flowering plants, which come and go as the season changes. Smaller pots can be filled with just one or two plants and placed around the larger ones. A pot capped with a fluff of alyssum or thyme is sensational. I love puttering with pots; arranging and moving them around is like setting up a still life for a painting. Brightly colored annuals in willow baskets arranged on an old garden table along the back border look absolutely smashing against the dark leafy shade of the woods beyond. And a big container filled with floppy herbs and trailing nasturtiums can rescue a garden from midseason doldrums while covering for summer fugitives.

Patio container gardens in Tuscan hill towns are often an exuberant horticultural collection of potted plants, hanging baskets, window boxes, and other ornaments, and inspired our kitchen herb garden. This small garden room, enclosed by the house and a lattice fence, is a stage for standards and topiaries, flowering annuals and herbs in window boxes, hanging baskets, and pots arranged on platforms of old bricks and flagstones. Mats of thyme, sweet alyssum, and winter savory creep around square and rectangular flagstones, and sweet cicely, *Artemisia* 'Powis Castle', monkshood, and lady's-mantle grow along the fence under climbing clematis, morning glories, and nasturtiums. This garden encourages artifice, whimsy, and spontaneity and always accepts my newest favorite plant. For reluctant gardeners or committed putterers, not ready to take on bigger spaces, a small garden room such as this, an extension of the house in sun or shade, should be especially appealing.

Good planting techniques ensure happy thriving plants. First of all, inspect plants for diseases and insects. We don't want plants in the ground or in containers to be dependent on problematic chemical sprays or time-consuming, often ineffective botanical sprays.

Loose, porous soil and good drainage are essential. As I am usually behind schedule, we use a commercial outdoor potting soil leavened with vermiculite or with builder's sand and compost, aiming for an equal mix. The important thing here is not to be intimidated by measuring out prissy recipes.

We usually pot up a lot of plants at once and mix enough soil for the job in a garden cart, as very efficient gardeners do. Before planting, soak the plant in a bucket of water for a few minutes. Then remove it from the grower's container and gently cut or tear off any encircling roots that can stunt growth and inhibit penetrating moisture. Line the bottom of the pot with gravel or broken shards to aid drainage, insert the plant, and cover with some planting soil until the crown of the plant sets an inch or so below the container rim (which makes it easier to water). Mulching with terra-cotta-colored pebbles or white marble chips will help retain moisture and prevent the soil from baking. Small pine bark chips are appropriate and effective for wooden containers. Water gently and shade the plant for a few days while it recovers from potting trauma.

Gardens facing south and west usually need a daily watering. Large pots and plants make more of a statement than small ones and also hold moisture longer. Plastic pots placed inside of terra-cotta pots, insulated with pebbles, polystyrene foam peanuts, or sphagnum moss cut watering time. Wooden barrels hold moisture for several days and are ideal year-round containers for ornamental trees and shrubs. Plants benefit from early-morning watering and the humidity of evaporating water, but such attentions in the midday heat can cause plant shock. When water seeps through the drainage hole, the plant has had its fill. Overhead sprinkling can cause leaf and flower damage and wastes water. Keep containers off the ground to prevent bug invasions, root rot, and mud splatter. Should a plant wilt from thirst, immersion in a bucket of water may restore its spirits.

One of my most haunting garden memories is of an empty Greek urn placed on a rocky outcrop high above Lake Como. I wonder about the gardener-dreamer who staged that unexpected and unforgettable image. Empty and beautiful pots artfully placed could be the answer for the gardener unable to oblige the peremptory quotidian routine of watering. I confess that when we abandon our container plants to the erratic and unpredictable ways of plant-sitters, we always lose a few, but then no one ever said that gardening was a low-risk proposition.

Unless plants get leggy and rangy, fertilize with an all-purpose plant food every two weeks. Slow-release fertilizer pellets and granules need too much note-keeping on which plant got what and when.

It takes a bit of trial-and-error experience to get the knack of container gardening and to exploit even some of its unlimited potential. There are so many plants to experiment with. I suggest just starting with some substantial leafy, textured plants and surrounding them with annuals, perennials, vines, and herbs suitable to the season and the microclimate of the location. Without guilt expunge any laggards, and don't even think of using little seedlings that have a long way to go. Summer's time is too short to waste coaxing and pampering, and there are so many wonderful and interesting plants to use as the seasons change from spring into summer and autumn. I try to keep a backup inventory for instant fill and renewal.

Experiment with compositions by arranging and rearranging pots, and try any plant that appeals to you. Just avoid the planting cliché (which should be outlawed) of any combination of begonias, coleus, geraniums, and dracena strangling in mats of variegated trailing vinca. Don't worry about fashionable color theories—if colors clash send one of the offenders somewhere else.

My garden journal reminds me every spring of last year's good performers as well as the unenthusiastic and ho-hum. It notes that I have promised to be more attentive to detail and to experiment with a greater variety of plants, even the demanding flowering pot geraniums—the prima donnas in all Italian container gardens.

So far in our microclimates, the plants in the following list are usually insect and disease resistant, drought tolerant, neat of habit, and good-looking. I have tried many more that need too much mollycoddling or are stress-prone in summer heat. I list plants here by their common names. Many are described in this book, but as most have several container-worthy cultivars, choice will ultimately depend on a little research in the garden centers. As memory fades over the winter, keep an account of your plants and their attitude and behavior.

Annuals and Biennials

Impatiens, heliotrope, flowering tobacco, forget-me-not, nasturtium, pansy, sweet alyssum, chrysanthemum, morning glory, moon flower, lantana, datura.

Bulbs

Lily, tulip, scilla.

Herbs

Artemisia 'Powis Castle', catmint, sage, mint, basil, chive, rosemary, parsley, thyme, myrtle, bay laurel, lady's mantle, lamium, scented geranium, hardy ageratum, and many more.

Perennials

Hostas, ferns, astilbe, ornamental grasses, and sedums.

Shrubs

Miniature and standard roses, box, caryopteris, euonymus, viburnum, hydrangea, cone-shaped juniper and spruce.

Vines

Clematis, English ivy, morning glory, honeysuckle, nasturtium.

On Garden Ornament and Other Matters

a bee diving into
a foxglove bell

Monumental garden architecture, colonnaded loggias, reflecting pools and fountains, spacious marble terraces, ornate balustrades, ponds, arches, pergolas, summer houses, follies, grottos, urns and statues of Greek and Roman immortals, and other ebullient detail belong to the history of western European gardens. Ornamental and utilitarian architecture and decorative objects are as integral to the history of gardening as the ever-changing fashions of horticulture and botany. From the Italian Renaissance well into the twentieth century, workshops of artists and craftsmen filled commissions to appoint the gardens of the rich and powerful with special site-specific projects and ornaments wrought from stone, terra-cotta, wood, and metal.

In the United States, during the last half of the nineteenth century, with fortunes generated by the industrial revolution, Civil War, and westward expansion, the newly rich acquired grand houses and grand gardens, establishing coastal and mountain resorts and suburban enclaves throughout the country. "Cottages" in the right resorts with showplace gardens evoking those of the great European (or even Asian) palaces and châteaux were a condition for acceptable credentials in a fast-forming new Society. It was the golden age of gardens, a brief moment in the nation's brief cultural history. Today some of these extravagant old houses and gardens, doomed by the changing social values wrought by World War II, are still maintained by private or government agencies and open to the public. Others have been converted into asylums, convents, schools, spas, condominiums, office quarters, or multiple building lots, their gardens annihilated or forsaken.

Though gardens today are more modest in size and scale, there is much we can learn from old gardens in this country and abroad about the use of ornaments and decorative architectural elements. These still add the finishing touch to most gardens. In the Northeast my favorite old gardens are in New England's golden age resorts: Newport, Lenox, Stockbridge, and Cornish. There are many different, interesting ways to use garden ornaments, and eventually one finds a style and a mood that makes a personal statement, right for the entire property and for life as we live it in this *fin de siècle.*

Nearly all gardens have something to teach, if only in certain details, and even unappealing gardens still help define our ideas and hone perceptions. We learn how to look at gardens, think about them, and ask questions: Why are some gardens smashing and others just ho-hum? What is it that lifts a garden, no matter its size, out of the ordinary and imprints its unforgettable image on our minds and changes our thinking? The ways of learning how to garden and how to paint are exactly similar. One learns how to do it by studying how other people have done it. We appropriate, reject, sift, and somehow find our own style and approach whether it is painting, gardening, or any other subject. I can think of no better way for gardeners to develop and refine their thoughts and intentions than by visiting as many gardens as possible. Many gardens have in one way or another informed my thinking and attitude about gardening and how to proceed here in our own gardening experiments.

Some gardens are extremely restrained and sophisticated, consigned to vast sweeps of lawn, an elegant *tapis vert* with trees and flowering shrubs, flowerless and without ornament.

Some gardens, quite the opposite, look staged for photo opportunities and seem self-conscious, affected, preoccupied with garden chic. Hoses are coiled with precision, pots and cloches are lined up by size, tools are perfectly arranged and displayed, and plants stand in weedless gardens like objects. A *mise en scène*, gardens like these, mannered and studied; the accent is on exterior decorating rather than gardening.

Some gardens sing for attention. On a recent local garden tour, visitors gathered to listen to the sound of music coming out of a rock. Investigation disclosed a loudspeaker installed inside of a fiberglass rock, spoiling, we thought, a horticulturally advantaged and rather posh garden of fancy roses.

And some gardens scream for attention. I think of one particularly, devoted to beds of tropical annuals and lawns littered with sundials, birdbaths, antique cast-iron railings, urns, and decorative objects. A bronze statue of a cherubic little boy rides a dolphin that squirts an arc of water into a vivid turquoise swimming pool. The startling spectacle, not light-handed enough to be amusing, trespasses on the long flat green fields leading to an eye-level horizon.

One of my favorite gardens is composed with herbs and brightly colored annuals, enclosed by a white picket fence and extravagantly and humorously outfitted with antique signs, benches, garden sculpture, birdbaths, and birdhouses. The gardener artist's insouciance and horticultural savvy miraculously save the whole scene from being cute or kitschy. It is an honest garden, reflecting the owner's passion for bright colors, a respect for the seventeenth-century house and its little garden, though without slavish attention to historical accuracy. Plants here thrive on the love and attention from their keepers and the homage of a steady flow of admirers. The entire property is one piece; house, gardens, lawns, stone walls, and fields weave together and merge effortlessly into the woodlands beyond.

The gardens of horticulturists, though rich in plants, are allegedly the least artistic of all as the emphasis is on botanical research—testing, analyzing, and documenting plant behavior. I have visited several deadly serious garden laboratories and so far I have to agree: nary an old pot or sundial anyplace. I think of one guru's garden to which worshipful cognoscenti flock and follow steps made of rubber tires down a steep hillside to view a sullen patch of experiments endangered by encroaching fields and woods. The entire property is cheerless, and a little touch of artifice would not necessarily violate its sanctity. But is there more here that doesn't meet the eye—is its esteemed keeper disclaiming fashionable and pretentious gardens, or is it really just the inartistic garden of a serious and dedicated grower who couldn't care less?

One of the most elegant and dramatic gardens I have ever seen was the grass-covered crest of a Tuscan hill where fluted terra-cotta columns topped with empty urns stood beside two wind-torn cypress set twenty feet apart, framing the distant view of the towers and spires of Siena. This garden and its keeper express the true meaning of "sense of place" by borrowing the landscape of this ancient and noble city and framing it in such an unexpected and understated way. But then, with 2,000 years of garden history to fall back on, why expect less?

The most inspirational gardens for me are ones in which flower beds, lawns, trees, and shrubs interlock and the whole is an integrated, harmonious sum of these elements. Ornament is spare and functional, accenting near and far focal points and leading the eye in and out around the property. Pots might be massed together or placed around individually to decorate bare places. Fences and walls are decorative and functional, serving as barriers or screens as well as support for climbing vines.

I like wooden tubs made from half whiskey barrels planted with large cone-shaped conifers to mark boundaries and entranceways. We place other tubs around the terrace with my favorite trendy plants. The blue-glazed containers we brought back from Japan looked better there with indoor plants, and though we use them in the kitchen herb garden for topiaries and standards, I think terra-cotta pots are more appropriate in New England. Sometimes certain garden ornaments are better left in the countries of their origin rather than inserted in an incongruous horticultural landscape. Ah, no matter . . . certain mistakes you can accommodate, and my blue-glazed Japanese pots are six of them.

Garden furniture: The options are to sacrifice comfort for fashionable status-symbol cast-iron antiques, or to compromise with the not-so-bad-looking lightweight, extruded aluminum, vinyl-webbed things that are guaranteed to last well into the next century. We like weightless furniture as our *fêtes champêtres* are movable and we are usually not disposed to give up comfort for style.

Every garden and every gardener needs a classic teak or oak bench as close by as possible. Our weather-bleached bench on the back terrace looking over the herb garden is a site for consultations with my co-gardener, lemonade parties with visiting grandchildren, and resting after aerobically intensive garden labor or just meditating, lulled by the happy humming of my garden pollinators gathering nectar for their queen.

I make platforms in the gardens with various-sized slate tops resting on piles of bricks on which to place significant empty containers or willow baskets filled with annuals. They are easy to make and easy to move around to try new compositions in a new setting to keep us from getting bored with the same old thing.

Pedestals with birdbaths or sundials and arches are classic ornaments. Birds actually do bathe and splash about in our kitchen garden birdbath, and the trellis arch with its climbing vines is a meeting place for single birds and also gives height and weight to the back herb garden.

Lattice evokes memories of old gardens and past summers and is used traditionally to construct summer houses, arbors, fences, and decorative treillage against a wall. We have a ten-foot-high fence enclosing the kitchen herb garden that supports hanging baskets and climbing annual or perennial vines, and turns this small space into a garden room. I would love to have a trelliswork gazebo but our *genius loci*, an advocate of "less is more," takes a dim view of the idea for the sense of this place.

Under night lights, gardens become magical and mysterious. Harry is always devising new theatrics for our terrace picnics with floodlights clipped to trees or posts or just stuck in the ground. On a midsummer floodlit evening flowers leap out of the night as the lights rake over the gardens, distorting shadows and cutting illuminated swaths through the trees beyond. We have a few permanent lighting fixtures but with an assortment of floodlights, heavy-duty extension cords, and some thoughtfully placed outdoor electrical outlets, my lighting designer co-gardener creates dramas and moods befitting different seasons and occasions. Too many gardeners overlook the pleasures of a well-orchestrated light show, sequences of lit and dark spaces across the gardens, lawns, and deep into the night beyond.

I think the whole property should determine the style and extent of decoration; on our land certain restraint is right and compatible with our tastes and dispositions. I like to experiment and try new arrangements, moving pots around making compositions in various places. With so many interesting and good-looking garden ornaments and decoration offered in catalogues and garden centers, the temptation to collect is insistent. Now and then I add one too many of something or other and the whole place will suddenly look cluttered. Gardening is often a matter of adding and subtracting—searching for harmony with the right proportions and connections so that ideally nothing can be added, diminished, or altered but for the worse. Well, I'm not there yet, but it's fun to think about: beauty, harmony, nature, perfection, and our individual inclinations and evaluations.

Gardeners learn to acknowledge the "sense of place": to let their property suggest the style of gardening, kinds of plants, and ornaments compatible and harmonious in relation to the surrounding fields, woods, or neighboring lawns and houses. Gardeners and their gardens take time to develop and find their own style, horticulturally and decoratively, and wise is the gardener who recognizes the *genius loci*—the distinctive atmosphere of a place and the impression it makes on the mind. And foolish is the gardener who ignores this guiding spirit, there in every garden to remind us that with garden ornaments and decoration less is more—well, most of the time, anyway.

Children and Gardens

lily 'Casablanca'

I cannot recall my grandmother's face, but I can always see the pink lady's-slipper that appeared one day near a goldfish pond in the damp shade of her garden. I also clearly see a small twiggy tree miraculously blooming with lollypops on Easter morning.

Gardeners can usually trace their interest and love of gardens to a special person, a special garden. I remember well my grandmother's wildflower garden where borders of ivy, lilies of the valley, and jack-in-the-pulpits meandered along under Japanese maples, dogwood, old oaks, and hickories. A split-rail fence and stone retaining walls defined the property, which sloped down a hillside to a large round mound or berm, crowned with the Chinese stone lantern that my grandparents brought from their compound in the western hills of Peking.

I would like to have the fugitive pink lady's-slippers someplace in our gardens, but only if they appear spontaneously. I suspect my grandmother borrowed her specimen from the woods nearby, but in those days gardeners knew little of endangered species.

Because of our foreign travels and the exigencies of moving our family around the globe so often, gardening was not on our agenda when our children were young. When we were home we spent our attention and energy beating back the invasive field and woodland plants that begat horticultural chaos around the borders of our property in Greens Farms, Connecticut. But we were granted visiting privileges to the garden of our friend and neighbor Hilla von Rebay, artist, art collector, and the first director of the Guggenheim Museum.

Getting there was half the fun—we scaled the back fence and made our way through a dense and dark copse of blue spruce that opened into an old field of wildflowers bordered with bramble and bittersweet. Then we crossed an expanse of lawn—a stage for rare flowering trees and shrubs—and picked up a path leading to the inner reaches of the formal garden. Hilla liked children and often with little advance notice invited us for afternoon tea. She presided over the ceremony in the terrace room, overlooking the shade gardens, always dressed in white silk. While she poured tea she spoke of many things—her memories of the bygone intellectual and artistic European culture, which she knew between the world wars. Conversational give and take was unimportant to her—we listened, mesmerized. Paintings by her friends and contemporaries, all early twentieth-century masters who once defined the avant garde, hung any old which way five deep on the walls. Her housekeeper came in and out replenishing Proustian tea cakes, sandwiches, and hot water.

Looking out across the gardens we could see the Italian Renaissance fountain, rose arbors, a majestic copper beech whose ancient branches swept the ground, weeping cherry trees, and a stand of ten-foot Turk's-cap lilies. Later, after tea, we might walk down to the shady terrace garden, through a pathway between clipped yew hedges and a grove of lilacs, into her spring garden where Oriental poppies, roses, iris, peonies, and lilies flowered in well-ordered and uninhibited exuberance—a garden designed by a visionary. These gardens were the first inspiration for my ongoing series of drawings and paintings of flowers and gardens, a subject matter that I have continued to explore and develop over the years.

One day her housekeeper called me to visit. I found Hilla, robed in white silk, reclining beneath a white canvas canopy and receiving friends in her beloved garden. It was my last visit—she died a few weeks later.

But it was Mr. Specht, her gardener collaborator, who understood, interpreted, and executed her horticultural philosophy and artistic visions, which made these gardens unique. He propagated and planted new plants and cuttings and kept the estate, its gardens, paths, walls, trees, and lawns, in good order. And if they disagreed, I have reason to believe he simply went about his own way and that was that.

He gave us rare plants and bulbs, and shared his gardens and his philosophy of gardening with us and many others who came and departed with a deeper awareness of plants and gardens. Mr. Specht stayed on for a few years until the estate was settled, but when he left, so did the spirit of the gardens. Shortly thereafter, we moved and began our gardening here, just a mile or so away from our old house.

Now that we and our children all have our own gardens, we think often of Mr. Specht, the gentle man who worked so naturally, so carefully with nature. For us all he was the special person in a special garden, and our first gardening teacher.

One of my greatest pleasures is taking my grandchildren by the hand and visiting plants around the garden—considering this one's appearance and that one's behavior. In the spring they work in the garden, and I assign chores that have a beginning and an end: "Please dig up all this hideous creeping Jenny and bury it under that tree." I think children should learn early on the value and rewards of work well done, and I escalate the wage scale established by their parents just a little bit.

Sometimes they just come to play; they might fashion landing platforms for the garden fairies out of flat stepping-stones, petals of columbines, daisies, coralbells, leaves of lamb's-ears, and unfolding fronds of cinnamon ferns. I find work to do nearby, the better to eavesdrop on the unselfconscious voice of childhood, so innocent, pure, and guiltless.

On Easter morning they gather here for Rabbit's Easter egg hunt. They find their baskets under a bush and the older ones lead the younger ones, following a trail of jelly beans and popcorn, which weaves aimlessly around the lawn, in and out of the garden beds. Every so often they discover little nests of straw filled with painted eggs and jelly beans hidden between rocks or under leaves. The trail leads to the big hole in the apple tree, Rabbit's house, where they uncover a cache of chocolate eggs hidden beneath pink and green shredded paper. But there is more—the trail continues, albeit haphazardly, and we come across a bizarre scene—abandoned stuffed rabbits and teddy bears lying about all over the place. Did Rabbit get tired, possibly even a little bored with the whole pageant, and just drop his Easter presents here, close to an old Chinese stone lantern in the hosta garden and a little twiggy tree with blossoms of paper flowers and lollypops?

the last of
Harry's roses

September's Garden

*S*easons are a state of mind—one gardener's early autumn is another's late summer. On this piece of real estate summer ends and autumn begins on the first of September. Actually, autumn begins almost imperceptibly in the middle of August: The collective voice of insects has a different timbre, the light lowers earlier in the afternoon, birds on their migratory route south pause to convene in the trees around our property, and falling leaves clutter the lawn. I imagine all gardeners are gently touched by melancholy as August wanes.

Garden chores in September are dictated by the need to groom out decay and dessication rather than curtail and shape exuberant summer growth. It is the time for leisurely consultations with my cogardener to plan next year's events, marking places for new plants and where combinations of plants will be rearranged. It is the time for critical assessments and reappraisals, moving or evicting plants that haven't lived up to our expectations. These are lovely, languid garden days. There is no sense of urgency, the pressure is over. We wind down, even dawdle in the warm September sun, watching bees, birds, and butterflies—thinking, dreaming, wondering.

I might never have realized the full dimensions and potential of a September garden, if a friend had not invited us several years ago to put our garden on tour for the benefit of a local charity. I had to accept this challenge, because it was there: part of my if-the-door-opens-go-through-it philosophy.

Before that summer, I had not realized that with a little planning, September's garden, surrounded by the flamboyant autumnal colors of fields and woodlands, rather than just fading away, could be a triumphant and dramatic epilogue to the summer garden.

Consequently, it was that summer that I became a full-time garden keeper in my efforts to keep the gardens in tiptop shape, primed for the big day, September 22. Neglecting duties one day meant overtime work the next. We stayed close to home, watering, weeding, grooming, planting, replanting, fine-tuning, fussing, and fretting. We declined the usual invitations to New England's offshore playgrounds or to anyplace that would keep us away for more than two or three days.

Any artist will confirm that in preparing for a painting exhibition, it is quite natural to worry and fret about this and that. Will you finish the work on time? What will people think? Will anyone come to the opening? Such worries are normal, but nothing compared to my apprehension thinking about several hundred garden inspectors poring over our modest accomplishment. I often awoke in the middle of the night unnerved by thoughts of Mother Nature turning unmotherly, even surly, and undermining all of our efforts with frost, rains, winds, or bugs. Perhaps more disquieting was a mental video of our gardens on visiting day without any garden inspectors at all.

Fortunately, sound and rational thoughts always returned with daylight, and I loved our gardens for just being and serving us well. I did not wish for much more, nor would I settle for much less. Our gardens suited our way of life, our priorities and commitment to gardening. They were pretty, sometimes beautiful, and we could keep them ourselves without hiring extra hands. I liked knowing that people would come here to see our informal gathering of plants. I would do my best to see that our gardens looked their best on tour day, and I suspected I was on the high side of a learning curve for a change, which was comforting.

September that year gave us a glorious accumulation of sunny, mild days, with just enough coolth at night to give the plants a little edge. On the appointed day, we betook ourselves to the garden shortly before dawn to effect significant adjustments: moving potted plants three inches to the left, four to the right, arranging garden tools and baskets artfully but casually in picturesque places, and inspecting each plant for imperfections—setting the stage. During the five years that we lived in Japan, I picked up some useful gardening tricks. Because gardens and stones are more alluring when wet, thoughtful hosts, to demonstrate esteem and respect for guests, water their gardens and stones before visitors arrive. In grooming a garden, the enlightened gardener leaves a few leaves around to demonstrate that man falls short of perfection. We watered all the gardens and left some leaves around.

The several hundred garden inspectors arrived—they came in drifts all day long. Time spent with gardeners is always nice, and this day was exceptionally nice. They love discussing plants and other topics germane to the subculture. They notice things that ordinary people overlook—certain combinations of plants, a new cultivar, new evidence of a bug blitz or the empty space just created by moving something. They offer sympathy where called for (malingering plants and other sorrows) as well as advice, praise, and encouragement. Do they carry magnifying glasses? Yes!

I uprooted perilla by handfuls for its many admirers and have ever since been amused by the notion of this comely fecund weed/plant, given a few years, carpeting Fairfield County with its iridescent purple leaves.

After the people left, I made the following entry in my garden journal:

The day was glorious—bright sunlight, deep shade. Our gardens surpassed themselves and all of the plants looked fresh, alert, and sprightly—the tall gangly ones leaning languidly over their neighbors for support. They all seemed to be showing off and actually competing with each other for attention. One lonely white-blossomed campanula and great clumps of goldenrod and monkshood held court along the stone wall border. Enormous clambering mounds of sweet autumn clematis climbing over the house got lots of attention, and so did the morning glory vines strangling the fifteen-foot stalks of cosmos. The back herb garden with the outrageous clump of interloping nasturtiums, dead center, seemed just about perfect with all the different textures, colors, and shapes playing off each other. Potting up lots of chrysanthemums to fill in spaces left by summer woebegones was foresighted, indeed, and I like to think evocative of Italian gardens. I will do much more pot gardening next summer.

The kitchen herb garden was a little plant-lined outdoor room, with the topiaries and standards staged on different levels, and clematis, nasturtiums, and morning glories climbing the lattice fence and trellis. The hard work all summer has paid off, and now I look forward to next summer and returning to a more relaxed mode of gardening without the pressing commitment of a garden tour. It was a fabulous experience. I think that I have advanced in my practice of gardening and that we passed our self-imposed gardening exam. I have a lot of new thoughts, ideas, attitudes, and plants to test next spring and much more confidence.

So, what are the attributes and characteristics of a September garden? Well, bloom colors are predominantly in harmony with the changing foliage of deciduous trees—in the warm range of reds, oranges, and golds. Rudbeckias, perillas, sedums, berberis, sunflowers, ornamental grasses, nasturtiums, marigolds, goldenrods, chrysanthemums, and zinnias all come into their own in September. Then the blues of monkshood, asters, eupatoriums, morning glories, caryopteris, and the whites and pinks of Japanese anemones, cosmos, roses, cleomes, Montauk daisies, boltonias, datura, feverfew, and phlox have all been waiting for their moment. The graceful giants, pokeweed, that have sneaked in behind the more aristocratic perennials and shrubs, spread their slender purple branches dripping with clusters of lustrous black berries, proving that one garden's dramatic accent is another's rampant, noxious weed, worthy only of annihilation.

And all of these enthusiastic autumn bloomers are supported by an elegant cast of herbs in their finest hour: artemisia, thyme, sage, nepeta, rue, tarragon, tansy, and others in their prime, ready for harvesting. Such are the last troupers of summer, a different-looking bunch, a little eccentric, and well worth the extra attention required all summer to keep them primed for this final act.

After September—then what? Not much as far as I am concerned. That's it. Enough. Time to go on to other things, here and abroad. During the next several months we put the garden to bed without a lot of to-do. We cut back some perennials, leaving the woody-stemmed and those with attractive seedpods to provide winter interest. We clean the gardens of dead leaves and other litter where slugs, bugs, and fungus could skulk over the winter. We repot and root prune some potted plants to winter over in our cold greenhouse; others, unpotted, will tough it out, heeled into compost. We clean and oil the tools and put them away with the pots (cleaned), garden furniture, and hoses. My co-gardener will plant hundreds of naturalizing daffodils and jonquils before the ground freezes. We reappear briefly after Christmas to cover the beds with two or three inches of salt hay, which will protect plant roots until early March—when the sap starts running and the birds pause in the trees on their migratory route north and spring comes again to these gardens.

Ecological Gardening

hemerocallis

G ardening is a national mania. The National Gardening Association in a 1991 survey reports that 80 percent of the 93.3 million households in the United States have one or more members involved in some form of gardening. In 1992 they bought $20.8 billion worth of plants and mowed, fertilized, and watered 20 million acres of lawn grass.

We read that these American gardeners are environmentally hip and that millions are involved in the new intergenerational "green" politics, working toward an environmentally safer world. They are represented by a new generation of elected officials alert to the damaged biochemistry of planet earth: global warming, ozone depletion, species extinction, toxic waste, and the loss or damage of forest, ocean, wetlands, waterways, desert, mountains, and agricultural ecosystems. Further they tell us that that ecologically cool gardening by whatever name— organic, naturalistic, regionally aware, "working with nature"—is standard practice.

Well, if all of this is so, what can we make of the following figures?

~ The average homeowner uses five to ten pounds of toxic chemicals per lawn—ten times more per acre than commercial farmers—for a total of 25 to 30 million pounds a year. (The overall use of pesticides dumped into the environment is 2.7 billion pounds every year.)

☙ Environmental studies show that gardeners use up 50 percent of the domestic water supply. An acre of lawn needs 27,000 gallons of water every week; and gardeners tend to overwater by 20 to 40 percent!

☙ According to the Environmental Protection Agency (EPA), yard debris accounts for one-fifth of landfill waste—about 31 million tons a year. Leaves alone account for 75 percent of the solid waste in the fall.

Something is going wrong somewhere because these figures hardly substantiate the claims being made about safe and responsible gardening by the new-wave gardeners, the composters, the native plant saviors, the drought-conscious, and the organic gardeners. Clearly, we need to review and reexamine our practices and try to do better.

International and national agencies, private organizations, and watchdog environmentalist and other special interest groups have to monitor the big national and global environmental issues, but we alone are in charge of our own backyards. While *they* manage the planet, *we* must manage our private places with informed and intelligent gardening. Every time we leave our yard waste in black plastic bags on the curbside we contribute to the enormous problem known as municipal solid waste. If we use toxic chemicals on our lawns, gardens, and trees, we contaminate the air we breathe, the ground we work and play on, and the surrounding ecosystem, as pesticides disperse into the groundwater, contaminating fresh-water wells and reservoirs. In 1987 the National Academy of Sciences warned Americans that 90 percent of all fungicides, 60 percent of all herbicides, and 30 percent of all insecticides may cause cancer. It is all up to us. We are the only ones to keep our own backyards safe—chemically free, for our children, ourselves, and the birds and garden insects in their complex and miraculous biological relationship.

Chemical substances control weeds, insects, diseases, and pests, and they can also pollute air, soil, and groundwater. The EPA has not evaluated many widely used pesticides, synthetic or botanical. One-third of our most commonly used pesticides were registered before 1984, when standards were less strict. There is great turmoil in the chemical industry and in the government about regulation of chemicals, including laws and acts protective of the environment.

Commercial growers have different problems from those of the home gardener, but they concern all of us. There is a terrible urgency to develop agricultural practices that are both safe and commercially viable, or there may be many more ecological tragedies like the Florida Benlate® disaster, a biochemical and legal mystery that began in early 1990, when farmers reported plant damage from Benlate, once one of the most widely used fungicides.

According to *The New York Times* of December 5, 1992, more than 1,200 Florida farmers have filed claims against E. I. Du Pont de Nemours and Co. for crops damaged or destroyed by Benlate. The Florida Agriculture Commission reports that the Benlate disaster caused economic losses of nearly $1 billion and that hundreds of the state's farmers had been ruined. Many growers and farm workers reported Benlate-related health problems. The product was pulled off the market in 1989 and the company was fined by the EPA. Benlate was put back on the market in 1990 and withdrawn again in 1991. In 1992, after spending $500 million to compensate farmers for crop failures linked to Benlate, Du Pont reversed course, rejecting any blame for the damage, and halted further payments. The liability claims were the most in the company's history, and the $1 billion losses were the largest Florida had ever experienced.

In August 1993 four growers in Georgia, Alabama, Michigan, and Hawaii reached an out-of-court settlement with Du Pont. After a five-week suit, with testimony running to three million pages of documents and 500 computer tapes, Du Pont agreed to pay one percent of the $430 million suit against them for actual and punitive damages.

The trial is of enormous importance to the company and the 400 other Benlate-related cases still pending around the country, to say nothing of the likelihood of expensive appeals. Du Pont officials claim a victory, and depict the growers who failed to prove their case as "greedy litigants going after a deep-pocket defendant." There will never be any real winners in these dramas, but in the meantime one wonders what exactly did cause the alleged $1 billion in crop damages in Florida alone.

The EPA evaluations on the carcinogenicity of many widely used pesticides, synthetic or botanical, are based on the manufacturers' long-term animal studies, which are then submitted to the EPA and appraised by a committee of scientists. The final decisions are by majority vote, which often muffles any dissident voices in the wilderness.

I don't think there is time to wait while they sort this all out. We independent home gardeners have no one to answer to but ourselves. We can eliminate pesticides now, whether natural or synthetic, and make our own backyard, at least, 100 percent safe for us, our children, and its future keepers. Is a weedless lawn more important than our children, our friends, and ourselves working and playing on toxic fields? Are photogenically perfect plants more important than the songbirds, insects, and little animals that visit our property?

Here is a summary of what we gardeners can do to nurture and protect the land we live on so temporarily:

⬥ Study your property and plant native species and their cultivars that are suited to your particular microclimates and topography. Plant disease-free and drought-tolerant species, and avoid plants suited to other regions and climates. Your state wildflower society and local Audubon and other nature centers can be helpful here.

⬥ Improve soil conditions by annual infusions of compost, humus, and mulches. Good tilth aids moisture retention. Mulch with living ground covers or bark chips to improve the soil, keep temperatures even, and prevent erosion, water loss, and weed growth.

❦ Compost—even small properties can spare enough room behind an attractive lattice fence, say, for two or three compost bins. Putting leaves and grass clippings in plastic bags overloads our dumps and is outrageously wasteful of leaves and landfill space.

 ❦ Look to your lawn and ask if it really must be completely weed-free. Mow high—two and a half to three and a half inches. Use a mulching mower (also called a convertible mower) to chop grass clippings and leaves that then decompose and fertilize. There are conversion kits for existing lawn mowers. Lawns need an inch of water a week. In droughts, grass turns brown. Don't panic and don't water—it is merely dormant and will recover.

 ❦ Can some of your property, even turf, become a wilderness area, a native plant conservancy, a natural field, or a bosky woodland place?

 ❦ If you use a tree service, ask for oil-dormant sprays for trees and shrubs as a preventive against insect pests. These horticultural oils have been around for a long time and are effective against a wide variety of pests in greenhouses as well as outdoors. They are relatively harmless to humans, mammals, and birds and do the job by smothering rather than by disrupting biochemistry, as conventional pesticides do.

 ❦ Reject plants that depend on spraying to control insects or disease. Good air circulation and clean gardens are essential. Eliminate weeds early before seed is set. Remember that insects are not deliberately destructive—they are just looking for a free lunch. A few less-than-perfect specimens do not ruin a garden.

 ❦ If you employ a lawn service, ask about its organic program. Use organic and natural fertilizers for lawns, trees, shrubs, and gardens. Several manufacturers sell complete natural fertilizers with various NPK (nitrogen-phosphorus-potassium) ratios for different soils and different regions. Some gardeners mix their own from natural sources such as bone meal, wood ashes, and dried blood. Japanese beetle grubs in the lawn can be controlled with milky spore disease, a biologically natural way that is effective within three years.

Our own small voices are muted by the roar of the eco-babble, but with a collective effort across the country we could create miracles just by practicing safe and ecologically responsible gardening. By keeping our properties poison-free, planting regionally suitable plants, and composting and conserving water, we can someday return the land we have borrowed from nature in better condition than we found it. This is the contract we should make with our gardens and consciences before all else.

Books

Joelyn's sunflower

Gardening books are essential to the education of a gardener, some more so than others. I enjoy reading them for their conflicting advice, opinions, and counsel and for their diversity of interests, emphasis, and experience. One gardener's rose garden is another's bug-infested briar patch. I like to consider these things even though the subject may be irrelevant to us and to our garden-keeping.

The golden age of garden literature coincides with the golden age of gardening—from the late nineteenth century to World War II, when gardener visionaries collaborated with the great architects, landscape designers, and plantsmen-botanists. With untempered idealism and no shortage of funds or labor, they were able to realize ambitious dreams and grand schemes, rearranging landscapes to indulge their fantasies. The early years, before the turn of the century, belonged to the amateurs: an eccentric, knowledgeable, self-confident, and opinionated crowd of men and women who really spoke and wrote just for one another and for the privileged few in the inner circle—botanists, horticulturists, the gentry presiding over the big estates, and their head gardeners.

These were also the years of the alpine and tropical plant-hunting safaris, endowed by well-heeled gentlemen botanists and authors. The seeds and propagations of their horticultural trophies would change the history of gardening, the use of plants, and the design and landscaping of space. Exotic tropical and alpine species extracted from their native habitats were pampered and coaxed to adapt to strange climates and conditions. Their introduction into the best gardens brought a merciful conclusion to that Victorian conceit, the bedding out of nonhardy annuals, and inspired the fashion for hardy perennial mixed borders. Imported exotics shared garden space in an admirable horticultural symbiosis with ordinary old-shoe natives appropriated from the cottage gardens of the peasantry, a style of gardening that has changed little in the last hundred years.

The draconian social and economic consequences brought about by World War II changed the history of gardening again. Estate gardening on the grand scale was no longer realistic or viable. Many of the great estates in the United States and abroad were bequeathed to the national trusts or broken into parcels and sold to pay taxes. Social displacement and economic forces severed the tradition of apprenticeship and training. The acquisition of skills necessary to maintain gardens, lawns, and greenhouses was simply not appealing to the postwar generation entering the labor market. The mid-twentieth century marked the end of one era and the beginning of another in the long history of gardening, as at the same moment Everyman was moving to the suburbs to build his dream house and make a little garden in the backyard. Gardens were within reach of every homeowner; they were no longer limited to the estates of the very rich (who were fast becoming less and less different from you and me).

Garden writing also changed, assuming a different direction, a different beat, and addressing a larger, more anonymous, less knowledgeable but expanding audience. The literature was no longer written by and for the horticulturally elite in the gardening world, but rather for the legions of new gardeners planting out the suburbs in the decades after the war.

These new gardeners are busy people, and they have less time to read personal chronicles of gardening experiences with their cranky, witty, and ironic observations. They want didactic, botanically explicit, horticulturally correct, hard core, how-to information. The bookstore shelves sag from the weight of this new subculture literature.

Many gardener/writers today appear enthralled by the postwar British school of garden writing, extolling ideal gardens where nothing awful ever happens. The critical eye, discerning mind, and partisan approach of the prewar writers have given way to descriptions of gardens where everything is always wonderful. Funny old black-and-white photos have been replaced with photographically opportune shots of improbable gardens where all plants are in full peak simultaneously.

There are a lot of how-to books written, I think, by people who don't actually garden. They are recognizable by their arcane advice, impractical suggestions, and overly ambitious schemes that assume funds, space, time, and labor are limitless. Many specialize in horticultural propaganda, with benumbing lists in Latin of plants for a broad and nonspecific range of climate and soil conditions. Desert gardening in California is without relevance to gardeners in New England. Unless a book is recommended by a trusted and savvy friend or reviewer, peruse it carefully before granting it space in your collection.

Still, the tradition of gardener/writers who take pride in well-written words and describe their own personal gardening experience with vivid imagery and profound feelings is not dead, nor is an audience that has time to read for pleasure as well as for information.

In the following section, I have organized garden books, rather arbitrarily, into several categories, which I hope will make selection easier for anyone overwhelmed by indecision, standing before linear yards of gardening books in libraries or bookstores. Chosen with discrimination, many books can, one way or another, make a serious contribution to the education of the complete gardener. A well-rounded collection could include a few from each of the following categories for reference, inspiration, or just the pleasure of a good read.

The Classics

The works of pre–World War II horticultural and literary persons, to wit: William Robinson, Gertrude Jekyll, Vita Sackville-West, Edith Wharton, Cecilia Thaxter, Alice Morse Earle, Louise Beebe Wilder, and Elizabeth Lawrence, for starters. These are impassioned English or American gardener/writers, to be read and reread as one's own gardening experience increases. They don't purport to teach the nitty-gritty of making and maintaining gardens, but they do impart interesting, amusing attitudes, observations, and advice as they provide insights into the minds of serious and dedicated gardeners. They are regarded as the sine qua non of garden literature.

Contemporary British Gardener/Authors

The prestigious cabal of contemporary British gardener/authors includes: Christopher Lloyd, Penelope Hobhouse, Rosemary Verey, Helen Dillon, and others who write encomiums to the art of national trust and estate gardening as practiced in England today. There is no shortage of British horticultural bias, attitudes, and prejudices, or of plant lists with many recommendations either unavailable or nonhardy in the northeast United States. These books are interesting, I suppose, to the experienced gardener who is well versed in botanical Latin and suspects that after Sissinghurst . . . there is nothing.

Practical and Specific Books

Invaluable to gardeners who want to know everything there is to know about a certain subject: plant families, certain kinds of gardening, integrated pest management, drip irrigation, landscaping, and much more. Many of these books are useful, relevant, and dependable. However, choose carefully. Books in this category can be ridiculous, with inane, incomprehensible charts and graphs that can be deciphered only if the book is turned sideways.

Encyclopedias and Reference Books

Several horticultural encyclopedias and reference books with A to Z information should be on every gardener's bookshelf. *Wyman's Gardening Encyclopedia,* Clausen and Ekstrom's *Perennials for American Gardens* and *Reader's Digest Complete Book of the Garden* are reliable reference books covering just about everything. *Hortus Third* is the mother of 'em all, a seven-pound behemoth, regarded by cognoscenti for years as the final arbiter in any significant botanical dispute.

Coffee-table Books

The books on photogenic horticulture, garden designs, exterior decoration, and historically important gardens, here and abroad, are wonderful coffee-table decoration. They are usually too big to hold, but they are good for flip-throughs, and the gorgeous photographs inspire sighs and dreams and ideas for future trips. Many add to our knowledge of garden history and make wonderful presents—even for the armchair gardener or traveler.

Trendy Books

The five-pound books by trend-setting, lifestyle garden writers whose gardens are a major part of their corporate enterprise are heavy and handsome, and exploit every aspect of gardening as practiced by their entrepreneurial authors. However, the beautiful English-inspired garden scenes in the photographs are not to be taken at face value by anyone without greenhouses, a few acres on which to practice, and a devoted staff to keep the scene photogenic.

My Favorites

My favorite books are by postwar American authors who really garden and care about the word, well written. They are books about gardening as well as garden writing, and they enrich the inheritance of garden literature. I think of Katherine White, Russell Page, Sara Stein, Roger Swain, Eleanor Perenyi, Henry Mitchell, Allen Lacy, Josephine Neuse, Sydney Eddison, Page Dickey, Michael Pollan, and many more. They write with a strong personal vision and a realistic experience and attitude about our own native plants and gardening in the United States, which is where our gardens are. They are valuable teaching books, informative, humorous, undidactic, and discursive, to be read and reread with pleasure, even excitement.

The list of suggested readings (page 249) includes these and other books that I have found instructive or inspiring for one reason or another.

The Education
of a Gardener

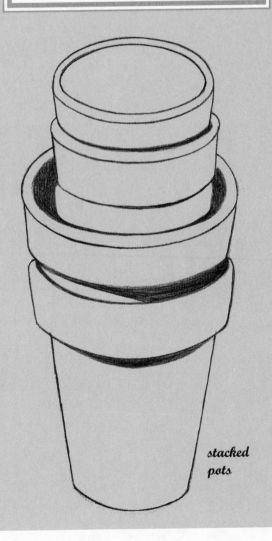

*stacked
pots*

While there are many ways to learn about gardening, there is only one way to learn how to garden, and that is to practice in our own backyards. We learn to garden by gardening, and the garden becomes the teacher. Somehow we muddle through this initial stage without extinguishing our own enthusiasm, figuring things out for ourselves with a few books and a good support group of gardening friends. We learn how to make and keep a garden, a triumph of hope and will over inexperience and even ineptitude.

It is an enjoyable process, this learning how to garden. We acquire experience, knowledge, and a critical sense by creating and maintaining a garden that actually survives our tentative, awkward ministrations and nature's pranky ways. We become familiar with plants and their names, habits, and customs. We learn to be philosophical about disappointments and successes. We learn to surrender impractical ideas to judgment and to delineate realistically our commitment to gardening. We learn that a garden is not a plant exhibition but a gathering of our favorite plants in a setting that we ourselves have fashioned with a little bit of luck, skill, humor, patience, and acquired knowledge. We develop the essential intuitive sixth sense that comes to all good gardeners in time, and we learn to let common sense be our guide. We realize that gardening is not an exact science, and we stop trying to control everything. We write down both names of every plant we grow. We learn that our supervision and presence should be light of touch and respectful of the land we borrow from nature; and yet as temporary caretakers of that land we must exert a certain amount of authority, know when to meddle and when to leave alone. We learn that the simplest effects are often those that defy money and ambitious effort and result from a balance of taste and knowledge.

We understand that we have a lifetime of learning to do in a field that includes botany, landscape design, biology, and the history of gardening—or civilization itself. One might just settle for a garden bed with a few plants and disregard all of this, but most gardeners find that the more they learn about the related aspects of gardening, the more enjoyable gardening itself becomes and the better their garden grows.

We learn how to garden by gardening, and we learn about gardening from classes, lectures, reading books and catalogues, visiting garden centers and other gardens and gardeners—all of which enable us to consider and evaluate new ideas and aspects of gardening and to determine our ambitions and priorities.

I have never been in a garden that did not have something to teach. Artists go to galleries and museums to observe and study how other artists solve certain problems, as well as to be inspired and possibly to appropriate a concept or an idea, something all artists do unabashedly. Years ago in a Lausanne gallery, I saw a small collage that inspired three or four different series of collages for me—ongoing projects for almost a decade. We never know when we might respond so deeply to something that it changes our values, perceptions, thinking, and vision—even our way of life. I get ideas and inspiration from other gardeners as I do from other artists. There is nothing wrong with appropriating and re-creating an idea if it seems right and feels natural to you.

Travel and visiting the great gardens of the world is invaluable to the education of a gardener. In any country, most major cities have botanical gardens and parks that are wonderful places to receive horticultural enlightenment and to study the universal standards of excellence, as well as to become reenergized.

For horticultural and artistic illumination some of the most inspiring gardens in the Northeast are projects sponsored by the Garden Conservancy. The Conservancy, founded in 1989, is a national organization that relies on public support to achieve its aim of preserving exceptional American gardens. More than two-thirds of America's great gardens have deteriorated from neglect and the battle lost against time and nature's forces. The mission of Frank Cabot, founder of the Conservancy, is to identify gardens as works of art and to preserve or restore them by facilitating their transition from private to nonprofit ownership and operation.

The Conservancy began its full-scale experiments with Ruth Bancroft's dry garden in California and Ambassador John P. Humes's Japanese Stroll Garden in Mill Neck, New York. This year it undertook the restoration and management of the John Hay Estate in Newbury, New Hampshire, and the long-term stewardship of the artist Robert Dash's garden in Sagaponack, Long Island.

Mr. Dash's garden, the only one we have visited so far, should be on every gardener's visiting list. He manipulates space on his two-acre canvas with a sophisticated multiplicity of interrelated horticultural events that wind and weave textures, colors, forms, and moods together in and out of merging and changing spaces. This is a master artist and plantsman at work, mindful of the illustrious history of gardening yet liberated from residual restraints and clichés.

The garden way first leads one past twenty-foot-high twisting tree trunks of strictly clipped privet, then slowly through shade and wild flower gardens, and across a Chinese bridge spanning a diminutive pond, where giant waterlily platters support fat sleeping bullfrogs under arching blades of water iris. Then we pass through a copse of specimen trees and shrubs, past a collection of glistening ornamental grasses, and down a rose-bordered red-brick walk that leads to the bleached fields beyond.

Next we are inside a tunnel carved through a stand of thick bushes. We emerge in an open space bordered by blueberry bushes and a tall privet hedge. We follow the path past box-bordered vegetable and herb gardens and four square brick-floored garden rooms, each with one large classic terra-cotta pot planted with flowing black-leaved sweet potato vines. Finally we duck under an arch of twined white-flowered hydrangea branches and into a walled garden of towering, billowing, flowering plants. On a stone bench there sits a collection of new plants waiting to be set out.

These magical gardens fulfill in every sense the mission of the Conservancy to preserve the best of American gardens as living works of art—"to live beyond their ephemeral nature and the mortality of their creators to be shared with generations of gardeners yet to come." For information about Conservancy projects call 914-265-2029.

Until 1991, when they became a publicly endowed foundation, the Stonecrop Gardens in Cold Spring, New York, were the private gardens of Mr. Cabot. They are a series of display gardens—a botanical museum demonstrating an encyclopedic range of plants in various microclimates and settings. The gardens spread over many acres, and visitors follow paths through extravagantly planted woodlands with ponds and ledges, several enclosed perennial gardens, and many more spaces with varied and particular horticulture—an educational resource for gardeners of all levels. For information about the Stonecrop Gardens, call 914-265-2000.

These are the sort of gardens that Harry and I plan our trips around—public and private gardens here and abroad. I love the eastern end of Long Island, the dark privet hedges, white fences, green lawns, and gardens carved from the old potato fields with flat faraway horizons. In those garden beds, blessed by sun and moist breezes, plants seem to grow with a ferocious energy. In the Berkshires we visit gardens created during that golden age of American gardening when landscape designers and their rich clients thought nothing of rearranging and sculpting the land to frame distant moody landscapes, or of draping gentle hillsides with gardens of tree peonies, roses, and ferns. These late Victorian gardens and summer cottages whisper of dilatory summer days—of times lost, lemonade and tea parties in the rose garden, porch-swinging, charades, and croquet. We also love to inspect the wonderful little town house gardens in Nantucket, Edgartown, and Block Island where hollyhocks and foxgloves bloom in tandem, santolinas stay crisp all summer, and rosemary, lavender, and thyme think it's southern France all over again. The sun shines, sea breezes cool these gardens, and some sunflowers touch the sky.

As the history of gardening has become more and more interesting to us, we plan our trips to France and Italy around well-known château and villa gardens. We depend on the kindness of friends, even strangers, to introduce us to private gardens and their keepers to see how real people govern their gardens. Gardeners enjoy showing their gardens, and a passion for gardening always leaps the language barrier. I can't imagine not having garden visitors—it would be rather like not exhibiting my paintings and just stacking them up against the wall.

In other gardens wherever they may be I sometimes see an image, a constellation of textures and colors that I would love to have, such as the long straight graveled path bordered by lavender and old stone walls that we saw in a Westchester garden, or the dry stone wall in the Geneva botanical garden with floppy and cascading sempervivums, alyssums, and other wall plants, or the irregular field of sunflowers in a friend's Long Island garden. They are enriching images but many will never leave the confines of my mind; implementing them would be hopelessly impractical for us—not doable. But someday soon I will plant hemerocallis along the stone wall bordering the field, and send a vine or two of clematis up that boring little tree near the grass garden. I forget what inspired these images—a pretty photograph or a garden someplace. It doesn't really matter.

What does matter is that our gardens are there for us to be in, to work in. My daily inspection tours reward me with variable artistic satisfaction and intellectual challenges, for these are the times when a merging of blossoms in the early clear light of morning or the dusky tones of evening may cause my breath to stop. At other times a certain section will suggest that we could do better with more of this or less of that. Gardening is a search for that elusive quality of perfection.

I love writing in my garden journal as the evening sun goes down and the bees are taking their last drag of nectar from carpets of thyme. On a winter night my journal is a pretty good read and reminds me of the yearly progress of the gardens as well as our own as gardeners. It is so easy to forget and so interesting to remember past triumphs as well as disappointments. Perceived failures or disappointments, an unrealistic scheme, overextension, or lapse of judgment isn't really a big deal in gardening. Even semieducated gardeners know that gardens are engraved in earth, not stone, and like a painting, gardens can be erased and without loss of face returned to sod with a sprinkling of grass seed. They know that time is never lost while taking flights of fancy and gaining experience. It is just and sound in a gardener's world.

Gardeners in their own gardens are artists, painting with plants, arranging space, and owe neither apology nor explanation to anyone. The students in my garden classes over the last three years confirm that while people may lack confidence about gardening, they actually have much more talent than they think. It is a question of replacing myths, mystique, and a lot of nonsense with a commonsense, practical, and natural way to garden. Within a few weeks of leaving these nine-hour workshops, they are designing and planting out sophisticated, realistic, and imaginative gardens. They are well on their way to acquiring the experience and knowledge for making and maintaining more gardens and have become passionate and enthusiastic gardeners.

I hope that this book, an elaboration of class material, will inspire and convince its readers that making and tending gardens is a personal and creative expression as absorbing and fulfilling as the study of any artistic discipline, and that gardeners are the masters of a unique and incomparable place—their own garden.

Suggested Reading

sunflower pod

American Horticulturist magazine, published by the American Horticultural Society, Alexandria, Virginia.

Bailey Hortorium, the Staff of the L.H., Cornell University. *Hortus Third.* New York: Macmillan, 1976.

Boisset, Caroline. *Vertical Gardening.* New York: Weidenfeld and Nicolson, 1988.

Brooklyn Botanic Garden. *The Environmental Gardener, Plants and Gardens.* Brooklyn, NY: Brooklyn Botanic Garden Record, 1992.

Buchan, Ursula. *A Bouquet of Garden Writing.* Boston: David R. Godine, 1987.

Clarke, Ethne, and Raffaello Bencini. *The Gardens of Tuscany.* New York, Rizzoli, 1990.

Clausen, Ruth Rogers, and Ekstrom, Nicolas H. *Perennials for American Gardens.* New York: Random House, 1989.

Colborn, Nigel. *The Container Garden.* Boston: Little, Brown, 1990.

Dickey, Page. *Duck Hill Journal.* Boston: Houghton Mifflin, 1991.

Druse, Ken. *The Natural Garden.* New York: Crown Publishers, 1989.

Earle, Alice Morse. *Old Time Gardens.* Detroit: Singing Tree Press, 1968.

Earth Works Group. *50 Simple Things You Can Do to Save the Earth.* Berkeley, CA: Earth Works Press, 1989.

Eddison, Sydney. *A Patchwork Garden.* New York: Henry Holt, 1990.

———. *A Passion for Daylilies.* New York: Henry Holt, 1992.

Fairbrother, Nan. *Men and Gardens.* New York: Alfred A. Knopf, 1956.

Foster, Gertrude B. *Herbs for Every Garden.* London: The Garden Book Club, 1976.

Gadol, Joan. *Leon Battista Alberti, Universal Man of Early Renaissance.* Chicago: University of Chicago Press, 1969.

Garland, Sarah. *The Herb Garden.* New York: Penguin Books, 1984.

Griswold, Mac, and Eleanor Weller. *The Golden Age of American Gardens.* New York: Harry N. Abrams, in association with The Garden Club Of America, 1991.

Hobhouse, Penelope. *Borders.* New York: Harper & Row, 1989.

Horticulture magazine, published by Horticulture Limited Partners, Boston.

Hylander, Clarence J. *The World of Plant Life.* New York: Macmillan, 1939.

Jekyll, Gertrude. *Colour Schemes for the Flower Garden.* Salem, NH: The Ayer Company, 1983.

Jekyll, Gertrude, and Lawrence Weaver. *Gardens for Small Country Houses.* Woodbridge, England: Antique Collectors' Club, Baron Publishing, 1981.

Keeling, Jim. *The Terracotta Gardener.* North Pomfret, VT: Trafalgar Square, 1990.

Lacy, Allen. *Home Ground.* New York: Farrar Straus Giroux, 1984.

———. *The American Gardener.* New York: Farrar Straus Giroux/Noonday, 1988.

———. *The American Garden Sampler.* New York: Farrar Straus Giroux/Noonday, 1988.

———. *The Garden in Autumn.* New York: Atlantic Monthly Press, 1990.

———. *The Gardener's Eye and Other Essays.* New York: Atlantic Monthly Press, 1992.

Lawrence, Elizabeth. *Gardening for Love.* Durham, NC: Duke University Press, 1974.

Lloyd, Christopher. *The Well-Tempered Garden.* New York: Random House, 1973.

McGourty, Frederick. *The Perennial Gardener.* Boston: Houghton Mifflin, 1989.

Mitchell, Henry. *The Essential Earthman.* New York: Farrar Straus Giroux, 1981.

———. *One Man's Garden.* Boston: Houghton Mifflin, 1992.

Nuese, Josephine. *The Country Garden.* New York: Charles Scribner, 1970.

Page, Russell. *The Education of a Gardener.* New York: Random House, 1983.

Perenyi, Eleanor. *Green Thoughts.* New York: Random House, 1981.

Pollan, Michael. *Second Nature.* Boston: Atlantic Monthly Press, 1991.

Reader's Digest. *Complete Book of the Garden.* Pleasantville, NY: Readers Digest Association, 1966 et seq.

Reinhardt, Thomas A., Martina Reinhardt, and Mark Moskowitz. *Ornamental Grass Gardening.* Los Angeles: HPBooks, 1989.

Rifkin, Jeremy, and Carol Grunewald Rifkin. *Voting Green.* New York: Doubleday, 1992.

Robinson, William. *The English Flower Garden,* 10th ed. London: John Murray, 1906.

———. *The Virgin's Bower.* London: John Murray, 1912.

Sackville-West, Vita. *V. Sackville-West's Garden Book.* New York: Atheneum, 1983.

Smith, A. W. *A Gardener's Book of Plant Names.* New York: Harper & Row, 1963.

Smith, Mary Riley. *The Front Garden.* Boston: Houghton Mifflin, 1991.

Stein, Sara. *Noah's Garden.* Boston: Houghton Mifflin, 1993.

Stout, Ruth. *Gardening Without Work.* New York: Devon-Adair, 1961.

Swain, Roger. *Earthly Pleasures.* New York: Charles Scribner, 1981. See also various articles in *Horticulture Magazine.*

Tanner, Ogden, and Adele Auchincloss. *The New York Botanical Garden.* New York: Walker and Company, 1991.

Thaxter, Cecilia. *An Island Garden.* Boston: Houghton Mifflin, 1988.

Tolley, Emelie, and Chris Mead. *Herbs.* New York: Clarkson N. Potter, 1985.

Verey, Rosemary. *The Scented Garden.* New York: Random House, 1987.

Wharton, Edith. *Italian Villas and Their Gardens.* New York: Da Capo Paperback, 1976.

White, Katherine S. *Onward and Upward in the Garden.* New York: Farrar Straus Giroux, 1958.

Wilder, Louise Beebe. *My Garden.* Garden City, NY: Doubleday Page, 1916.

Wyman, Donald. *Wyman's Garden Encyclopedia.* New York: Macmillan, 1986.

Index